MW00804131

SUSIE

Sue Funk

ISBN 978-1-64300-194-4 (Paperback)
ISBN 978-1-64300-195-1 (Digital)

Covenant Books, Inc.
11661 Hwy 707
Murrells Inlet, SC 29576
www.covenantbooks.com

FOREWORD

I 've been praying about why I have felt the need to share the positive and the negative parts of this story. I started out with writing only the positive and left it alone for two years and now have been prodded by the Lord to write it all, even if it seemed terribly negative in many areas. I have felt like a traitor over sharing some of the negative things about bad choices I have made and my parents have made, and I've prayed about it overstepping my boundaries in respecting them. Of course, isn't that what the spirit of family secrets does to a person? Make them feel guilty and like a traitor?

I have come to the decision that if it will help someone else to see how God forgives and how God saves, this whole project will be worth it. The sins of the parents are visited off to the next generation and the next if we don't come to realize that we can break that cycle. It is a costly price to the kids of the next generation.

This story tells of how I have come to know Jesus Christ as my Lord. He is the Savior and Deliverer of these many generational sins in my life and my family line. This is a story dedicated to the next generations of my family and to the last two or three generations of families who have had a life of ease, being handed everything they could ever want whether they needed it or not, sometimes to the tune of financial ruin. It is because of that saying that goes like this: "If you always do what you've always done, you will always get what you always got." The finances have been put into a bag with holes and have disappeared through being spent on drugs, alcohol, gambling, and many other vices that only the readers know.

There is also a scripture that says, "What a person sows that person reaps." There is also another side to this saying. Children have a tendency to reap what a parent sows, which points to the gen-

3

erational curses that I have been talking about. The scripture that says the sins of the parents are visited off to the next generation is what we are seeing when children reap what their parents are sowing. These children grow up and start sowing these same curses into their children, who are the next generation that reaps. I am writing this to warn about the sowing and reaping law: I do not want my kids to reap what I have sowed. I have also seen this curse business skip a generation and then continue working in the next generation.

God does not have grandchildren, which means that when a child grows up, he or she must have developed a relationship with the Lord for him or herself in order to stay under the shadow of His wing. Coming to know the Lord personally brings a person face-to-face with forgiveness and love that covers a multitude of sin and places them into the loving hands of a living Savior.

If this country keeps going the way it is going, there might be a major move toward losing all of what I call clutter in our lives that keep us from seeking the Lord. A day is coming when calling on Jesus Christ for help is going to be the only way of escape.

The scripture in Jeremiah 29:11 has been misquoted when a person doesn't include verse 12 and 13. It says, "I know the plans I have for you says the Lord, plans to bring a person prosperity and not disaster. Plans to bring about the future you hope for." We read this verse of the scripture and go for it. Or we are told that this is what God wants for us, and we leave out the next two verses. We have taught our kids that God is like a Santa Claus and if we are good he will take care of us. When a child grows up and learns that Santa Claus isn't real, God must not be real either, and the lie goes on and unbelief strengthens and reigns. We wonder why we aren't prospering, and we go from one disaster to the next.

At some point, we start begging God for help when nothing else works. Verse 12 of Jeremiah 29 says, "Then you will call to Me. You will come and pray to Me, and I will answer you." Verse 13 says. "You will seek Me, and you will find Me because you will seek Me with all your heart."

These disastrous events in our lives cause us to have a great need that brings us to the point of calling on the Lord. He is our only hope for the future. Please start calling on the Lord for help!

This need in my life for God and my answering His call is what saved my life.

I pray that this book encourages each reader to press on to know the Lord. God will and can redeem anything and anybody. He will come. A person will never be disappointed.

When we don't have a relationship with Christ, our choices are focused on what is happening here on earth in our average of seventy-year life span, and we think there is no existence after death. In reality, our lives here are the beginning of eternity for each of us. We choose how we are going to live, and it will have an impact on our eternal existence. The reality of eternity can have an influence on our lives and choices here. We need to evaluate our lifestyle from an eternal perspective, and we might find ourselves prioritizing and choosing to live differently.

This book has been in the making for a very long time.

Last night, I asked the Lord what he wanted to call the book. He said to call it *Susie*. That is a name that I was called by my many childhood family and friends. I thought *Survivor* or *Survivor to Overcomer* would be better, but I guess submitting to God's way helps a person to overcome. In all my decisions, I have found that it is better to submit to God's way of doing everything I put my hands to, and it will cause me to have a rich and full life.

Chapter 1

I have to start with a funny thing that happened to me a few weeks ago at the Bozeman, Montana, Walmart. A little five-year-old girl came up to me while I was in the process of buying fabric. She wrapped her arms around my leg and said, "Grandma, I want that." She pointed to a bolt of beautiful blanket fabric with princess designs on it. I'd never seen her before in my life, but was so touched by her that I said to her, "I would love to buy you a piece of this fabric." I thought that I would buy her enough of the fabric for a comforter and proceeded to pick it up and head for the lady who cuts the fabric. As I looked over my shoulder, I saw her sister who was standing beside her with the look of "Me too." I thought, *Great, no problem!* I would also buy the sister enough for a comforter. My husband just moved to the end of the row and watched to see what was going to happen next. My husband always handles these little situations that seem to always happen to me in public places so wonderfully.

I asked the fabric lady to cut each of the two little girls a yard of the material that I thought would be enough for each of them to have a little comforter. As she was cutting the fabric, the youngest little girl went into a total temper tantrum. She was screaming and crying, "I want all of it!" I was wishing that I could do that for her, but at $7.99 a yard, the whole bolt was thirty yards and cost more money than I had. She just kept screaming, and her mother just stood there not knowing what to do. After the first piece of fabric was cut, I just ignored the little girl and went to her sister and wrapped the fabric around her and started oohing and aahing over how beautiful the piece of material looked on her.

Kind of reminds me of what the Lord does for us, as I read the scripture in Romans 11:14 that says Paul oohs and aahs over us hoping to provoke his countrymen to jealousy in order for them to be saved.

The older sister played the part perfectly until the younger sister decided that the cut piece would be okay. We headed for the checkout counter to pay for their fabric.

The little girl reminded me so much of me at her age. I was born in Sheridan, Montana, and was the third baby born in the new hospital that was an old house on Mill Street, belonging to Dr. Rossiter.

Dr. Rossiter was the doctor who attended my birth and was a mentor for me from that time until he died at an old age. That old house later became a secondhand store that made for a good story. Being born in a secondhand store was the way my childhood seemed from the time I was born. I always fought the feeling of being second-rate and secondhand. I was always the last one chosen for sides in a baseball game at school. I didn't get it that I was probably a lousy baseball player. I took it as a personal offense. Living with this constant feeling of not measuring up caused me to strive to be someone that I was not.

I just couldn't figure out who this someone was, but it wasn't the person who I was. This continuous striving was a root cause of anxiety and was a cause of illness in my life. I was born a strong-willed child just like this little girl in the checkout line at the Walmart store.

I remember crying all the time because things didn't go my way. I soon learned that things weren't going to be going my way either. I went into survival mode, which later the Lord had to break me from in order for me to learn to become dependent on Him, not myself.

This survival mode is what I call stuffing everything that bothers me and pretending it doesn't exist until the pressure from the anxiety caused me to fly off the handle, so to say, or to break out bawling just like I did when I was little. I have learned to smile on the outside when I am happy or sad on the inside. Sometimes I have to literally tell my face to let go of the body language it has learned so well and give up. Let Jesus have his way.

CHAPTER 2

And now I will introduce myself.

My name is Sue Funk, but the name I really like to go by is Dolly Pardon Me. I am married to John, alias Johnny No Cash, and we have delved just a little (actually not enough for me) into a clown ministry called Dolly Pardon Me Ministries.

I remember looking at pictures of one trip that we took to the Watch program and the prison at Gaylen, Montana. I just laugh at the one picture taken at McDonald's in Butte in our crazy costumes as we are getting coffee. I have crosses and scriptures that I hand out to all the interested people who are curious about our mission. The Watch program is in an institution that helps reeducate alcohol and drug abusers who have been constantly in trouble with the law in hopes that they can be reintroduced into society. The prison houses kids who have done everything from murder to robbery to you name it and they have done it.

The ministry at these two places consisted of John playing his guitar and me playing the blowiano as I call it. It is actually what they call a melodica. Ronda played the Djembey drum. We played music and gave testimonies to the prisoners and saw a wonderful response from men and boys, of which many repented and asked to receive Jesus Christ into their hearts, which was overwhelming. I just love doing this.

We have also spent time using our gifting at a few rest homes and retirement centers. Another time of ministry was going to Virginia City, Montana, during the busiest time of the summer and playing music on a street corner and walking up and down the boardwalk playing "Jesus Loves Me" to every tourist. There wasn't a single rejection. I played that song 250 times that day and saw men crying while they stood there listening and then we prayed for most of them.

One young man with two little kids stood and sang the song as I played it. His two little kids just stood there, and he told them to sing. They said they didn't know the song. He said, "Sure you do. All kids learned this song in Sunday school." He then realized they had never been to a Sunday school. The man looked at me and announced, "I think it's time I took them," and he promised he would.

Another miracle that happened that day in Virginia City started the night before. While I was sleeping, I had a dream and was given direction for what I was to do the next day. There is a restaurant in town that has an outside veranda where two men play very dark music while the patrons would eat their meals. I dreamed the night before that I just walked up and started playing music with them. Then I told the two men, "Now it's my turn." In my dream, we played the song "Mine Eyes Have Seen the Glory of the Coming of the Lord." I said to the Lord, "If you want me to do what I saw in the dream I was willing."

The next day, as we were walking the boardwalk, I was praying for the right timing for all this to happen. As I walked by the veranda, the two men were playing some song on their guitars, and I felt that this was the time. I just walked up and started playing my blowiano with them. I have an ear for music, and if I can read a person's lips, I can play right along with them and that is what happened.

They said after that first song, "How about this song?" Yup, it went good. So they tried another song, and it went well. Then I told them that now it was my turn. I started playing "Mine eyes have seen the Glory of the coming of the Lord."

The two men started playing along, and one of the two men ran over and got his harmonica and started playing it. The people who were eating started singing along. As people were walking by on the street and hearing the music, they stopped and started singing the song too.

And the spirit of God fell in that place. I could see a change in those men, and God showed them that there is good music that blesses. It changed their hearts. They begged me to stay and keep playing, but it was time to move on.

CHAPTER 3

I love Virginia City because that is where I grew up.

After World War Two was over, soldiers returned home, and the celebrating began. My father was one of these soldiers and miraculously came home in one piece.

My parents married at that time, and I was soon part of life in Virginia City. Living in a small town of 150 people usually consisted of spending a lot of time at the family meeting hall called the Tavern Bar or the Pioneer Bar or Bob's Place or the Bale of Hay Saloon.

My mother had nine kids, and I was number three. I was the beginning of the second family. I was the oldest of seven but still a middle child. I have an older brother and sister who split their time between living with us and living with their father usually several states away.

I seemed to have been born to become the mother and father of the younger kids and also the parent to my parents much of the time at a very young age. I thought I could cook, iron clothes, clean house, and take better care of the younger ones that caused much conflict between my mother and me.

I remember the first meal I cooked, which was at the great age of four. My older brother Pete and sister Lea Anne were living with us at that time and were at school. My mother was still in bed because of the time spent at the family meeting hall the night before. I decided that my younger sister Sally and I needed food. I found a frying pan full of grease on the stove, which I proceeded to turn on. I broke a few eggs into the pan to make scrambled eggs. For some reason, a half full pan of grease doesn't do a very good job of mixing in with a few eggs to be scrambled. At that point, it became such a mess that

I got scared and just put the hot pan on the floor on the side of the stove and moved on to making toast for us.

That night after my parents returned home from the family meeting hall, my mother proceeded to drag my older sister, brother, my younger sister, and me out of bed to stand in the kitchen lined up until whoever made that mess and burned the floor confessed. I was too scared to confess, and my older sister was the one getting the blame but kept denying it. After what seemed like half the night of standing there getting grilled, I finally confessed to the crime, and I can't remember what the discipline for that was but I hated looking at the black spot on the floor beside the stove for the rest of the time we lived in that house. I was more careful how I cooked after that.

That old house was a very scary place to live. When I was in charge of the kids and something fearful would happen after dark, like the basement door blowing open, I would have visions of mountain lions coming into the house or strangers, which gave me sudden fear. In fact, these situations terrorized me. I handled these times by taking the kids to one of the bedrooms upstairs and pushing the dresser in front of the door for our protection. We all crouched under the bunk bed for the night. I never revealed the terror I had because I wasn't willing to pay the price of how this problem would be solved, which I will reveal in a page or two. I counted the cost, and the price wasn't worth paying. The terror was also stuffed deep within my heart.

My mother could depend on me as I was a born enabler. I was so young I had to stand on a chair to cook and iron, but it was a great challenge as far as I was concerned. The more I did, the less my mother did, which freed her to spend most of her time at the family meeting hall. She did come to know the Lord before she died. And much forgiveness flowed between us. It is amazing to remember the difference between the mother I had as a kid and the mother who changed when she was old and lived alone. She tried to make up for all that happened by coming to a few of our sons' football games and sitting with me in the cold. She would drive her little car that my brother Jon gave her the twenty miles down the valley from Virginia City to Sheridan where the home football games were played. I found out that she loved football. She never said that she was sorry for what happened to us as kids, but those little times we spent together sitting on that bench in the cold covered with blankets to keep warm meant so much to me and I knew that this was her way of saying she was sorry.

My mother decided to quit smoking in her early sixties to give me a birthday present because she knew that it would make me happy. It was also her way of showing me that the change in my life meant something to her. She was also having health issues caused by those foul cigarettes. She made it for two months but finally gave in to the temptation to start smoking again. I was so blessed that she even tried but was so sorry that she couldn't overcome. That was the best birthday present I could ever have even if it was for only two months. If she could have stayed off those defiling things, she might have lived for many more years. I remember visiting her and finding out that she fell back into that terrible habit of smoking. She said that she just couldn't give up her friends. Ya right. Everybody needs friends like that. She got to the point where she could hardly breathe and had to sleep sitting up. She finally had a stroke one evening and was rushed to the hospital in Sheridan where she died. It was amazing that she was able to use the phone when the stroke happened, dial my brother, and even though he couldn't understand her he knew it was her and knew she was in trouble. He rushed to her house and found her and called the ambulance. As my brother and I sat with her through the evening, I read scripture to her and prayed for her, and that was what seemed to calm her as she slowly slipped away. I knew that she went to be with Jesus.

My mother was so young when she passed away. As I look back now thinking about when I was the age she was when she died, I was still a girl at heart. The drinking and smoking steals a person's youth. I do thank the Lord for those few short years before she died that we were able to spend the time that we spent with each other. I got to know her a little. She had such a good personality that I didn't get to see when I was growing up because she was too busy with her life. We both missed so much.

CHAPTER 4

My father just lived in his own oblivion and paid little attention to what went on in our lives as we were growing up. He was the favorite ragtime piano player who played music in all the bars up and down the valley, and the local patrons encouraged him and built him up and filled his head with pride and added to his entrapment.

There were times when the parental parties moved from the bar to our house, and I was sexually assaulted by one of their friends when I was four years old. The bathroom was upstairs and down the hall that passed by our bedroom, which made for a perfect side trip for that perverted man. That is probably why I started putting the furniture in front of that bedroom door when I was babysitting the kids.

A teenage boy also assaulted me several times when my mother hired him to babysit, which gave me the guts to convince my mother that I could babysit "just fine" at age seven. The parents would try to do what they thought was right by getting a babysitter once in a while. I had to convince my mother that it was okay. We didn't need a babysitter. She couldn't afford it, and I couldn't deal with the consequences. There was no way of ever telling my parents what happened because that just isn't what is done when you live in a home like the one I lived in. I was too afraid of being blamed for it happening and being disciplined harshly because of it if I told anyone. I was sure that my parents liked that perverted man more than they liked me. He would dance an Irish jig by himself in a drunken state while my father played the piano. The parents spent more time with him than they did with us.

This really was the beginning of my learning to stuff all feelings to survive.

SUSIE

There is a picture of me in the first grade sitting in the back row at school, and I had such a grievous look on my face. I look at that picture and remember the reason why. These reasons caused much fear and trials for me during those years throughout my childhood.

CHAPTER 5

They say that a person is as sick as their secrets, and there was much secretive sickness in my growing-up years in Virginia City. Oh ya. That town isn't the lovely town that so many think. Actually, the town is lovely. It's the kind of people who lived in the town who were the problem. I'm amazed how we who have left had such an addiction for being in Virginia City that it was miserable getting it out of our system. I was addicted to it, and my first year of marriage almost didn't survive because of that addiction.

I just saw a video about girls being trafficked, and it made me think that it wasn't much different in my life. What I went through was nothing compared to what trafficked girls go through, but it's all the same pain. I would say negligent trafficking happened to me for free, not even for a price.

One of the biggest secrets of Virginia City was the pedophile who owned and operated the local grocery store. All young girls were warned to avoid going into that store, but there wasn't a person who came forward to put a stop to his seducing every little girl he could entice into that store. They just kept the secret and allowed him to keep coaching the high school basketball team. The pedophile's wife knew what was going on, but she taught school and dealt with her frustration and anger by treating the little girls in her class as though they were mongrels. She was the teacher I had when that picture was taken. As I think back on this, I'm sure that that poor woman suffered terribly, not knowing what to do.

When I was in my thirties, there was a Virginia City school reunion that was being planned, and it was told that, that couple was going to be in attendance. That was the first time I had to start allowing the stuffed forgiveness to start coming out of my heart. I couldn't deal with being in the same town with them at that time, so I couldn't go to that reunion. It grieved me so much, and I am still working on getting through the pain that these people caused me to go through. The first step of healing starts with a person being able to talk about it. And if someone starts talking about it, many doors will be opened for others to also begin the healing process. We *aren't* the only ones who suffer these things like we think.

I go through the "I forgive" process and pray for healing of the pain it caused, but it still sneaks up on me from time to time. I know that God can even forgive and is willing to forgive them as I forgive them. God has to. I wonder what happened to them for them to get into all this bondage. God comes to us by conviction, asking us to repent and forgive those who hurt us so he can forgive and cleanse us of all unrighteousness. The devil wants to keep us in bitterness, anger, and condemnation forever. Satan hates us. God loves us. I wonder how Jesus felt when he was hanging on that cross. Because of what Jesus did for us, our destiny is now able to change. We have been given the permission to use the pain that we have gone through for good in order to help others who are still suffering from this kind of pain. Even though men have evil intentions, God works all things that have been put upon us together for our good, we who choose to walk in God's ways. God is the same yesterday, today, and forever.

I have always been amazed at my dearest childhood friend who suffered to an extent that I never had to suffer. Her stepfather came home from the bar at night earlier than her mother, and she was raped over and over by that evil man. It still amazes me how she came to forgiveness for what he did to her. She is a strong Christian woman today. This is what God wants for us to become, a bridge from the darkness of this world to the light of the Lord. We can be a bridge to help someone else that has suffered in this way but haven't found the way.

Forgiveness is the answer. Before I came to know Jesus, I used to make fun of them (godly Christian people), and now I am one of them. This was a turning point of my brokenness. I'm on the road to finding forgiveness for my sins. I have faced these issues, which is the beginning of breaking the cycle of fear.

You wonder why I write this personal information. It's because one in three girls and one in four boys to this day are suffering from these same things in this country. I want them to know that there is hope. There is no safe place on this earth to leave a child to fend for themselves! Yes! Even in a small town of 150 people! My older brother and sister through these years spent much of their time living with their father, and they never seemed to be around when times were at their worst in the family. Thank God for that. When things got too bad, they were shipped out to go spend time with their father. I don't know the things they went through when they weren't living with us. I can imagine that things weren't too easy for them at their father's either.

My older sister overcame the issues she had to deal with and has been married to the same man for over fifty years and has three beautiful daughters and many beautiful grandkids. She went to college and became an engineer for a major business while in the middle of raising her kids. She overcame.

My older brother got married young, spent much time serving in the marines and three terms in Vietnam. He was one of three brothers who served in that terrible war at the same time. The youngest who was also a marine was killed. He came home, went to college, and got a teaching degree and taught industrial arts for years and then started his own business achieving so much in developing land in Washington. He and his wife raised two beautiful smart kids who are highly educated. Their daughter gave them two beautiful grandsons. They overcame so much.

I have a sister who lives in Alaska who owns a restaurant in Soldotna and lives a life of overcoming also. She raised four beautiful kids who are now raising their own families, giving my sister grandkids and great-grandkids, and overcoming is the name of their game.

My brother who is a beautiful finish carpenter lives in Virginia City with his beautiful wife. They have three beautiful daughters and two grandsons. They live next door to my beautiful little sister and her husband. She is a nurse's aide at the rest home in Sheridan. She raised four kids who have overcome more than their share of tough times. They all spent many a year at our house overcoming the situations that have tried to take them out. They all overcame. Then the baby girl of the family retired from forty years of hair dressing and graduated to become a cook at the same rest home in Sheridan. She has two beautiful sons, grandkids, and a husband who loves her very much. We have overcome, I would say. We didn't grow up to be victims of our environment. We overcame.

CHAPTER 6

I was a born mother. At the age of seven, I would, in the evenings, run two doors away to the public library and get books to read to the two younger siblings. And that was a feat in itself. I would run down the yard and jump the fence into the alley. Then over an iron picket fence in pitch-black night keeping my eye on the bright outside light hanging on the side of that huge granite building to keep from getting into fear, I would open that heavy door and give a quick look at the shelf of kids' books, sign the card, run out into the black night, and be back to the house where we lived in a matter of not too many minutes. There are so many of the fairy tales that kids hear that were many of the books that I read. They were the most terrorizing stories that I ever read, and I was cured from ever reading them again. I was never tempted nor manipulated into reading any of these books to my own kids. I wouldn't read most of those ungodly stories to a child.

There was one book that affected me in an amazing way. It was called *The Princess and the Pea*. That book somehow gave me hope that someone somewhere would find me and help me find what my true calling was in life. I knew that I was worth more than the way I had been treated. The person who found me was Jesus Christ. And he will find you too if you just start calling his name. He's actually just waiting for you to give him permission to be part of your life. Then he lets us be a part of his life, which is wonderful.

During this same time in my life, my younger sister Sally and I decided one night to sit on the stairs and wait for our parents to come home from the family meeting place. After growing up calling our parents "Betty and Harold," we decided we wanted to have parents like other kids as maybe this would help us to become accepted for who we were. We really wanted to be loved like what we saw happening at other kids' houses. It might have been a false reality of what we saw, but it looked better than what we were living at our house. We decided to call them "mom and dad" when they came in the door, but we lost our nerve and ran to our bedroom when we heard them coming in.

CHAPTER 7

It took coming to know the Lord as adults before we could break that bondage and begin calling them mom and pop. But it was a hard one to overcome. We also learned to hug them and kiss them in their later years. We were never kissed or hugged once by them in our life as kids growing up. I am sure that they were also never hugged or kissed in their lives either. My mother grew up as a little rich kid who was put into boarding schools and was farmed out to neighbors. She told me how she was terrified of her grandfather. Her father died when she was twelve, and her mother moved her to different places as she got a college degree in order to get a job. My mother inherited her grandfather's holdings, which amounted to a lot of money, and she squandered it quickly, living the lifestyle she chose to live.

We did learn what love was by the dogs and cats that we were constantly dragging home to love and nurture. There were many sets of kittens born in the closet in an open drawer or on a pile of our clothes that never seemed to make it into the drawer or onto a hanger. My brother brought home a huge black lab whose name was Mack. This dog was amazing. He could open the front door in the middle of the night to go out, but never learned how to close it behind him. It soon was twenty below zero in our house just like it was outside. When my older brother had to go spend a winter with his dad, the dog had to go with him. They decided it was time to come back home from Idaho to Montana, and without permission, my brother and Mack hitchhiked back home. He was in the fifth grade. They made it. And I thought I'd never hear the end of my mother screaming at my brother when he walked in the front door with that dog.

There was a pond that we called the swimming hole off in the draw above town along the road that took many people to the top of Alder Gulch. We spent many a summer day swimming there with Mack the dog and any horse we could connive out of our uncle. Some spring days, I remember breaking the ice off the edge and going swimming. I guess that was our way of hurrying up summer.

CHAPTER 8

*W*hen I was in the fifth grade, we lived in that eight-by-forty-two trailer that we moved back from Canyon Creek to our grandfather's yard in Virginia City on the lower road across from Daylight Creek. I received a pair of beautiful cowboy boots as a reward for babysitting the younger kids that summer. Those boots disappeared, and I never knew what happened to them until one day not too long ago when my sister Karla told me the story about wearing a pair of cowboy boots down the middle of the creek. She got stuck in mud up to the tops of the boots and couldn't get the boots out of the mud she just extricated herself from the boots and left them there.

I also received a hula hoop for Christmas that year, and the highlight of my remembrance was when our neighbors who were two teenage boys whose names were Dick and Don Bullock spent an afternoon practicing learning to use that hula hoop while standing in the street. I was an expert at the process of making that round piece of plastic keep twirling around my waist. I taught them how to move their hips to keep it from falling to the ground.

Now that I have interjected a couple of happy incidences not including losing my beloved boots, I will go on to what I was discussing earlier. John, my husband, made up for my loss by buying me a pair of boots that looked just like the ones I lost as a kid. These boots are part of my Dolly Pardon Me ministry attire.

CHAPTER 9

*T*here were a few other instances that happened also that I needed healing from. My aunt had a high school boy living with her, who I thought was supposed to be safe. He came from the Twin Bridges Orphanage to play basketball because Virginia City didn't have enough kids to make a team. He convinced me to go for a ride with him when I was thirteen, and in my innocent naivety, I got into the car and went with him. Before I knew it, he had driven to a secluded place off the highway about five miles from town and proceeded to try to rape me. I got away from him, jumped out of the car, and ran. He chased me and caught me by my jacket, which I unzipped and let fall off me and I kept running as fast as my legs could run. He ran back and got his car and tried to run me down, but I got to a safe place behind some sagebrush. It was about twenty degrees below zero that Christmas vacation, and without a coat, I got very cold as I ran back to town; and when a car came up the road, I had to hide for fear that it was him again. I finally got home without freezing to death and found that I could run like the wind. I was very sorry about losing that beautiful gold jacket that my aunt from Butte had given me for Christmas the week before.

My parents never noticed that I was still going without a coat and never asked what happened to that gold jacket. They were in the middle of their own overdramatized life. This situation was a tough lesson for me to learn, and not being able to tell was another crime, as that person needed to be dealt with before he did kill someone. He left the valley soon afterward and never came back, which I was thankful for. I'm sure that he was waiting for the hammer to fall. I know that there were angels there protecting me. In fact, I think that I would be surprised at how many times angels are doing their job. The scripture in Hebrews chapter 1 verse 14 says that angels are ministering spirits who serve God and that they are sent by God to help those who are to receive salvation. I learned much from that situation. I became more wary of who I got into a car with.

At that time, it was very hard to deal with being told that I wasn't old enough to date men after all of my early years of being told that I had to be a big girl and do the job of an adult. I was thirteen for God's sake. Rebellion was the price I paid. I remember my older brother Pete deciding that he was going to take over ruling my life and convinced my mother that the two of them were going to take me to the sheriff's office for a tongue-lashing and warning that I would be put in jail if I ever went with another guy. Now that was a challenge. At least the sheriff didn't beat me and I continued doing what I wanted. I learned to be streetwise and careful of whom I did spend my time with.

Summers in Virginia City started off with a celebration to open all the displays of the old buildings that were a hundred years old. They had a parade and a reenactment of a hanging of one of the road agents who were buried on Boot Hill. The actors in this production were the local people dressed up as cowboys, road agents, and the posse who caught the guy that was going to be hung. My uncle who had the horses for rent on main street would play the drunk who rode his horse into the bars in the middle of the thousands of tourists and was caught and dragged to the place where he was hung.

Then the partying began for a summer of constant drama everywhere a person looked. Tourists came by the droves and filled up that town from one end to the other. We learned how to be hosts from a young age. The kids from town were the guides leading tourists on horseback to all the important sights around town. Other kids had jobs in the information center and helping with teaching tourists how to pan for gold. If a kid didn't have a job, they just invented a job. We learned all the details of the history about the town and the area around town to entertain anyone who was interested enough to listen.

We met famous people who came through town. We met foreigners who were enthralled with every aspect of life in an old historic ghost town. The first time I ever saw a nun was in front of the grocery store. There were these women who were dressed in long black dresses and looked just like the characters in the books like I had read to my younger brothers and sisters. I thought that they were witches who came to town. They scared me so totally that I ran home and hid.

CHAPTER 10

*N*ow getting back to when I was five. I knew what age I was with each situation that happened because of which house we lived in at the time. We moved to Butte for a short year when I was five, and it was such a relief to get away from all the dysfunction. There was a little more normalcy in our lives. I thought that I found what heaven looked like. I later remembered the scripture in Revelation about the streets being paved in pure gold clear as crystal. We lived on Phillips Avenue, the street located behind the Emerson School, which was in the process of being paved. Roadwork wasn't like it is now when a street is paved. At that time, there were five-gallon buckets of tar everywhere up and down the street, and some were opened and half full. My younger sister Sally and I decided to get into those buckets and sit down and relax. We came out pitch black. After going home, I found out that Butte wasn't heaven, and those streets of black gold caused me to get the tar beat out of me literally.

While living in Butte, we all came down with every kind of measles there was. Sally ended up with what the doctor called scarlatina, which meant that Sally had to spend six months in bed because they said it could affect her heart. I think that she did end up with a heart murmur from that. Spending that much time in bed didn't work too well. It took all of us to keep Sally in that bed. She needed constant entertaining. I missed much of that school year from being sick. Sally and Jon weren't in school yet, and Karla was born that fall and was the new baby in the house. LeaAnne lived with our grandmother in northern Montana that year, and Pete also was with us. The tiny house had two bedrooms. One bedroom was for our parents and the new baby, and the other bedroom were for the rest of us. I won't forget the constant problem with finances that followed us to Butte. The bill collectors were constantly knocking on the door. The house was a constant disaster, and one morning, the owner came to collect the rent. We were always warned to never answer the door, but Sally at this time must have forgotten and ran to answer the door. The drama that stands out this time was that Sally was wearing a pair of my mother's dirty underwear on her head like a hat. That man left dramatized I am sure, and my mother took the rest of the day getting that situation out of her system. I loved living in Butte because the drama was a totally different kind of drama.

My mother also took me to a dentist whose office was across the street from the bowling alley a few blocks away. My teeth were rotted out of my head, and the dentist was horrified. He humiliated my mother so much that we left that place and never went back. I suffered from aching teeth for many years. Between rotten teeth and back pain, I suffered much. I constantly got terrible eye infections at least once or twice a year. We thought it was from being allergic to cottonwood trees, but it was part of the health issue I suffered, which was a genetic one.

Butte was a place where a kid could walk for blocks and finally end up back on the block we lived on. I was always taking Sally for walks, and one day I lost her. I went back home and forgot to tell my mother that I lost her somewhere. My mother finally realized she was gone, and before the night was over, the whole town was looking for her. She was three years old. They finally found her at the fire station on Harrison Avenue. There was a beautiful park called the Columbia Gardens that was built by the huge mining company that hired most of the men in town. This park had a roller coaster, merry-go-round, and swings that kids could spend days playing on. The flower gardens were dazzling. We spent much time at that park the summer we lived in Butte. There were little grocery stores every few blocks to buy food, and a truck came every other day and delivered milk to our doorsteps.

This was also about the time a television station began broadcasting in Butte, beginning at five o'clock each afternoon. My mother purchased a television for us to watch to entertain us in the evenings. The station started with "The Star-Spangled Banner" and then the test pattern and then a program where we guessed shadow shapes that looked like animals. If we could guess what it was, we called the station for a prize if we were the first to call in. They broadcast all evening before signing off for the night. I liked living in Butte.

We lived in Virginia City most of the time except the year we moved to Butte and the year we lived at the Canyon Creek phosphate mine, which was near Melrose.

CHAPTER 11

*W*e soon moved back to Virginia City from Butte, and the chaos that was more familiar to us. The story that I remember that happened at this time of my life was the time that my brother in the fourth grade and my older sister in the sixth grade were back home with us, and we all got into the car that was parked on the side alley by the house we lived in. My brother was backing the car up into the main road and back down to the parking spot and back up into the main road when we saw old Judge Bennett coming up the road in his car. He lived in the house across the alley from us. We all ducked down to keep him from seeing us, and the car rolled forward down the alley until it hit the garbage barrel and knocked it over. The front end of the car was lifted up and high centered over the garbage can. My parents had to get a wrecker to remove it. My older brother said that my father asked him if he had some money, and my brother did, as he always had spare change from odd jobs. My brother told my father how much he had and was ordered to hand it all over. My father told him that if he was going to take up driving he was going to have to help with the expenses of keeping the car running.

That was a good lesson for us all. I always had thoughts or maybe nightmares of that car driving by the garbage barrel and rolling down and hitting the library/museum lawn fence, going through it, down the lawn, and over the rock wall. It wasn't in the wintertime so there wouldn't have been a snowbank to make for a soft landing. My mother decided that my father needed to spank my older brother for some God-awful thing he did. I will never forget my father taking Pete up the stairs and hearing Pete scream like he was getting killed. Finally, my mother went to check on what was happening. She caught my father clapping his hands and telling my brother he'd

31

better scream. The fight that ensued from that display was settled. I think my father could have gotten a black eye from that incident.

We were raised to live in a pretend world and were told that what happens at home stays at home. We just went on living as if things that happened didn't happen. I was always in trouble because of certain older women in town who would pump me for information of what was happening at our house for the gossip wheel, and I just blabbered it all. Of course, I then had a sick feeling in the pit of my stomach waiting for the hammer to drop. And it usually did. When things got too hot because of threats from the welfare department of us being removed and put into the Twin Bridges orphans' home, my mother just packed us up and moved us, which was the reason for the move to Butte until things cooled off.

And we continued to pretend. We also moved to Canyon Creek because of the same pressure. One other move to get us off the streets of Virginia City was just to take us up to Harvey's cabin near Summit, about ten miles up Alder Gulch, and dump us for half of one summer. That was an experience in itself. We couldn't stray too far because of the moose, and we couldn't sleep at night because of the pack rats. We did try to walk back to town a time or two, but a moose was always on the road that caused us to turn around and run back to the cabin. My parents were in and out, but not very often.

They replenished the supply of peanut butter and jelly and bread and cold cereal and milk. I should be thankful that we did have food to fix for ourselves to eat. We kept the milk in the little spring that flowed down the draw alongside the cabin. Of course, there were always cans of beer that were cooling in that little spring. We learned what it felt like to drink that stuff and how to puke. I liked it much better in town where I could do whatever I wanted. I felt like I was trapped in a two-mile radius and couldn't stretch my legs at that cabin. I was used to having a ten-mile radius to run in.

This cabin up Alder Gulch was really an amazing place to stay. Across the road from it was the ghost town called Summit, which is at the head of the gulch. There was a dredge boat that came up as far as Summit in the 1800s digging up the landscape and leaving piles of dirt and rocks from this point down the draw as far as the town of

Alder, which was twenty miles away. I still wonder what it looked like when it was a lazy creek wandering down through this area instead of those piles of rock for twenty miles. Those rock piles did have many little ponds hidden in them that fish could spawn in, and the fishing was tremendous. We as kids spent many hours fishing in these ponds. It is amazing to think that a hundred years before my time, my great-grandparents were part of this event of mining gold. There were thousands of people living within these twenty miles between Summit to Alder. Farther up behind this cabin that we stayed in, set into the hill, was a trail that at one time went to an old gold mill that had fallen in. This was also part of our playground where we lived that summer. There were actually two cabins side by side, and between them was an old mine that we were warned to stay out of. The temptation to go into it was always resisted because of the fear of it coming down on our heads.

We were too young to have known how to look for artifacts that were probably plentiful in that area. I can still see in my mind's eye my relatives who lived up and down this draw in the many mine cabins that sat beside the tunnel and the dump where the men worked raising their babies and riding in and out on the wagons pulled by six and eight horses filled with the proceeds of what was removed from these mines. There were several old cabins still tucked in above the road along the way down the draw. There was a couple who lived in a cabin a few miles down who played music in town most weekends. In fact, if I remember right, they were pretty famous musicians from the old vaudeville days in the big city. Their cabin was pretty high class compared to the other cabins up there. She even had an old piano that she played in the living room. They wintered up there many winters when I was a kid but moved to town because of getting too old to fight the snow. He had a mine shaft behind his cabin also. There was an assay office in Virginia City that the gold nuggets were taken to and exchanged for money to go to Stephen's Mercantile for another grubstake of supplies to take back to the cabins and also for a new batch of what they called hooch. Their excuse was that it kept their blood from getting too thick, and the prescription was at least a glass or two each night before turning in. There were men and couples and families living in many of the different mine cabins up Alder Gulch, Brown's Gulch, and many no-name gulches. Some of these people only came to town when they were totally out of supplies. Others were in town every night. Many of them looked pretty grizzly, and many stunk like they hadn't had a bath for months.

CHAPTER 12

I loved the little old ladies who seemed to live in every nook and cranny in the town of Virginia City.

I have counted them, and there were almost forty of them, each living in one of the run-down shacks on every street. I don't know how they didn't freeze to death in the wintertime. Several of them had a few chickens living in the backyard, which helped with their having something to eat. This was before the day of Social Security checks coming in once a month. There was the welfare department, but these proud ladies would starve to death and die before they would take a handout. They were almost all tall and skinny, which is so different from the older ladies of today.

One of the richest ones was the lady whom we called Aunt Ollie. She had a brother who lived in her upstairs who was a recluse. He had his own door to get outside, and he only came out in the middle of the night. He slept all day and walked the streets at night. He wore a heavy trench coat almost to his ankles whenever he came out, summer or winter. Aunt Ollie would put a plate of food on the stairs where this old guy could get at it once a day. I remember when she realized that he probably died after not getting his food for several days. She was afraid to go check on him for fear of what she would find. I was always the kid who was hired to help clean up messes like what he left, and I was horrified. Aunt Ollie had a dog that I got the blessing of feeding when she was gone on a trip or to see her daughter who lived in Butte. I was so afraid of that dog that I would open the can of food and throw it over the fence for him. I was supposed to check on her house also. While the dog was eating, I would make a run for the front door and get inside and slam the door as fast as possible.

Aunt Ollie was a hoarder, and her house showed it. She had enough beautiful dishes to serve the Queen's staff and a dining room table large enough to seat them. Everywhere a person looked was nice antiques and tons of knickknacks. She had an armadillo body, which guarded her guest living room. Aunt Ollie would hire me to wash her dishes every week or two when she would finally run out of dishes to cook and eat with. I remember cleaning her bathroom one day, and the toilet was so bad that I used Purex and ammonia to get the grime off. The Purex was okay, but the ammonia didn't mix too well. After crawling out of that house and almost fainting from the smell, I suffered from a terrible sore throat. I learned a hard lesson there. I decided that I was allergic to working for Aunt Ollie.

Aunt Ollie was a gambler and gave me some punch cards to sell around town to win a gift like a stuffed animal. I would go sell these and bring her the money. The last one she gave me to sell was to my demise. I had a pocket full of money, and Ranks Drug Store was too much of a temptation. After spending the money at the drugstore on candy, I was then too afraid to go back to Aunt Ollie's. I didn't know if I was going to live through that episode.

Another older lady lived across the road from us in a two-story house that played along with Sally and me when we would trick or treat her several times a year. Her name was Clida Batten. I will never forget when her son drowned in the Ennis Lake. I felt so sorry for this lady. She seemed to always be alone and sorrowful.

There was an old lady who lived across from the church whose name was Etta Burns. She lived in a cold barren shack that amazed me. She was one of the few ladies who always had a cookie for us. Her son lived with her when he wasn't in jail, and he had these wild frightening eyes. My mother hired this lady a time or two to babysit us. Her son would show up and terrorize us. One time, he came in a drunken state and climbed to the top of the pine tree in our yard. I remember his mother screaming at him to get down. When I would walk downtown, I would forget and walk down the sidewalk on the side of the courthouse where the jail windows were. Her son was one of the men in jail who would be looking out those bars and yelling. They scared me terribly. I didn't think of just going down another street so I crawled on my hands and knees to get by where they were. Ahhhhhhh, I laugh just thinking about that.

I would go visit Velma Farmer who lived in an old house where the train depot now sits. She was a jolly old woman who laughed a lot and always had cinnamon rolls to feed us. She was one of the only heavy women I can remember living in town.

Going around the corner to the back street was another great place for a treat. There was a couple whose last name was Galigar. They lived in the house that squaw Mattie lived in before she died. Mr. Galigar was ill and lay in a bed in the living room while Mrs. Galigar puttied around taking care of him and cooking. She had a gravelly voice and talked a mile a minute. She was a pretty caring lady. Going up that back street, I remember Mrs. Ellen Walker who lived in the two-story house on the creek below the Fairweather Inn. Mrs. Walker was antisocial. I don't know how she survived. She didn't have chickens or a garden. Maybe she saved the money she earned when she was young to live on.

The next old lady was Cora Finny who lived above Alta Butler and across the road from the Vickers Place, which sat just under Boot Hill. Cora loved to have visitors. She didn't have much to eat but could entertain us for hours. Alta, on the other hand, had a few chickens in her backyard that laid a few eggs, which must have been what she lived on. Alta seemed to be always depressed. She never invited us in to visit. Aunt Lucille Dixon lived in the next house going up the street. She was another hoarder who had a house full of supplies for her hobbies. She could walk faster than anyone I knew. She always had a bunch of chickens that were loose in her yard. She had a great garden, and I'm sure she fed many of the old women who lived around her.

There was always something happening at her house. She had an old washtub that she soaked and washed wool that she scabbed from the sheep ranchers from down the valley. She would wash and rinse and hang gobs of the wool on her clothesline to dry. Then at slow times she would hand card that wool to make quilts, which were the rage of the town. Everyone wanted one of them. She taught me everything she knew about how to prepare the wool for a quilt. The knowledge was good for me as I became a sheep rancher and used what I learned from her. I learned from her how to knit and crochet. She didn't have much room in that little run-down house of hers but could always get a huge quilt frame set up to make quilts. She had a knitting machine set up and made wool socks for gifts. She also had a piano and an organ in that little house. I was born with music in my bones, and she encouraged me to learn how to play. I had a few accordion lessons from her, but dragging that huge accordion we had to her house was a chore for a little tiny girl whom the wind could have easily blown away.

Mrs. Dudley lived in my great-grandmother's house across the road from my grandfather. My great-grandmother sold this house because two of her sons died in the 1918 flu epidemic, and she decided she needed to get out of there. She bought a car with the proceeds and left. I always looked at the history of my great-grandmother with amazement. She came to America from England, living in Lockport, Illinois. She met my great-grandfather there and married him. He soon left for the gold fields of Montana, ending up in Twin Bridges and working at the Round Barn, which is famous for raising racehorses, before moving to Virginia City because of gold fever. After getting set up in Virginia City, my great-grandfather sent for my great-grandmother and their baby son to come to Montana. She rode the train to Salt Lake City and then took the stagecoach to Montana. They lived a hard life at Granite Creek working the land to raise crops to sell to the miners who lived up and down the draw. They raised a pile of kids, and then my great-grandfather died.

My great-grandmother moved her family to this house in Virginia City. She also bought the land where my grandparents' house was later built. And the whole hillside was hers where most of her kids lived after marrying. Her daughter Annie who was my grandmother married my grandfather Carl Burgstrom, and they lived across the alley. Her daughter Sadie lived in a little house behind my grandparents. Aunt Sadie had a beautiful butterfly collection of local butterflies she caught. It was a sight to see. Beautiful. When I was fourteen, I realized that Aunt Sadie had what we called hardening of the arteries, and her memory was shot. I started taking care of her the best that I knew how to. I brought her home with me and fed her. She had gotten so skinny from not knowing how to get a meal that she ended up being taken to the rest home in Sheridan where she died.

CHAPTER 13

I remembered as a kid that my siblings and I would all be thrown into the little 1954 Ford station wagon to head for home after spending the weekend in Virginia City. We would travel to Butte for groceries on our way back to our home in Canyon Creek, which was a phosphate mine near Melrose, Montana. We lived in an eight-by-forty-two-foot trailer house that was set up in a flat spot alongside the Canyon Creek. This was a place where my father had a job working at the mine.

I could never figure out why the car could never pass a bar as we traveled through the towns on the way. The car would instantly stop, park, and the parents would jump out, saying, "Stay in this car. We will be right back." They sometimes returned within an hour or two. It was always an all-day and an all-night trip to get home. It's amazing how we survived. Some weekends after spending the time in Virginia City, we would head back to Canyon Creek late at night on a Sunday night. We would go over a dirt road, which was a cutoff road from Twin Bridges to Melrose. The corners were wicked, and we had several close calls. The constant drama that causes underlying stress was always a part of these little trips.

One night, my father was passed out on the rider's side as my mother drove. He accidentally put his foot on the gas pedal, and we almost missed getting around a very dangerous curve as the car sped out of control. I woke up to my mother screaming at the top of her lungs for him to move his foot. I don't know how she made that trip as inebriated as she was. I still remember that terror. Situations like this cause a person to have posttraumatic distress. I remember a time when we were going to Butte from Canyon Creek and a patrolman stopped the car and told my mother to get control of those kids. Sally and Jon were both sitting in the window, hanging out over the side as the car was going down the highway. There was no such thing as seat belts in those days. That I'm very sure is when myriads of angels were dispensed from heaven to protect all of us. That cop let her keep going after she got those backseat windows rolled up. And the tongue-lashing went from the cop to her to all of us. And we all just stuffed it and went on our way. Oh well. If we didn't have constant drama, we would think something was wrong. I now wonder how people live like this, and a large percent of people do live like this year in year out.

CHAPTER 14

*W*hen I was in the third grade, we moved to the Canyon Creek mine near Melrose, where my father worked. That was a year of all years because we hauled our water from the creek behind the trailer that we lived in. The toilet worked as long as we had a bucket of water to flush it. My father dug a hole alongside the trailer about seven feet deep with a shelf at about five feet that we laid boards across and then we filled back up with dirt. The bottom two feet was about six feet across, and the top five feet was about eight feet across to give a foot on each side to lay the boards. Then we put the sewer drain down into this hole. And the toilet would flush, and we could use the sinks.

Sally and I used a large stick or the broom, which was put through the handle of a bucket, and we each took a side to bring the water to the house from the creek. We showered at the public shower house on Friday nights where the miners showered after work. That little creek was a great place to skate on that winter. Sally and I would skate down that creek onto the Big Hole River. We only had the guts to go a short way out onto the river, as we instinctively felt the danger that was there on that river. As I think about it now, I shudder.

We rode in the back of a jeep truck that was used as a school bus to go to school in Melrose, which was eight or ten miles from where we lived. Sally was named Friday sickness because every Friday she got sick and puked all over all of us in the back of that truck and we went to school smelling like puke. I'm sure the reason for that was we were out of food by Friday and got tomato juice and crackers for breakfast, which was the culprit. I was nicknamed Super Baby by the other kids who rode on that bus. It always graveled me, and I hoped that it was because I was super and not a baby. I must have acted like a baby and bawled at everything. We would go to the local Duck Inn restaurant for lunch, which consisted of a bowl of soup every noon. There was another family of kids that we picked up in the jeep bus. These kids didn't have the money for lunch and would go to the Duck Inn with us and order a cup of hot water. The waitress always had the catsup sitting on the counter with a basket of crackers, which made a great cup of free tomato soup for those poor kids. I never forgot that and was always sorry.

I saw a lab dog standing on the side of the road every day for a week while riding on that bus, and every day I begged the driver to stop and let me get that dog. He finally relented, and I brought home a beautiful female lab dog who was about to have puppies. That dog disappeared before the pups were born, and I later found out that my mother got rid of her because of not wanting more responsibility. I was so brokenhearted. That dog was going to replace the loss of my calico cat that I had to leave in Virginia City when we moved. I had combed the town of Virginia City looking for my cat before we left to no avail. They were both major losses in my life.

A brother whose name was Henry Thomas was born December 31, 1956, while we lived at Canyon Creek. My mother took him to the hospital in Butte because he was terribly sick with a bad cold, and he died of what they called double pneumonia on February 14, 1957. We had no heat in the house that week before he died.

We moved back to Virginia City at the end of the school year after his death. On November 24, 1957, Victoria Ann was born, only to die a terrible death on February 22, 1958, which I will talk about later. I remember after these two incidents I was walking down the street and saw my mother walking up the street with a maternity shirt on, and I was in total shock and felt terror. I made a vow that another baby wasn't going to die because I would take care of it. I was so angry at my mother for letting this happen. After I came to know the Lord, I had to learn the first lesson of forgiveness. The scripture that says honor your parents if you want long life hit me hard after I came to know the Lord, as I was in the early stages of not honoring my parents and judging them, which is only the Lord's job.

I'm sure that I suffered from the same shock that soldiers suffer from because of the things I have had to deal with.

Kathleen Marie, "Kitty," was born March 16, 1959, the following year. She was the last baby born to this family and she lived.

CHAPTER 15

That fall, my father was in a mining accident that nearly killed him. My father was bringing a loaded mine car out to dump over the edge of the mine dump, and the car didn't stop. It just went over the edge rolling over and over to the bottom of the mine dump with my father going over also. At the hospital, they told my father he would never walk again or move his arms or legs. They loaded him up and brought him home and dumped him in bed. No insurance and no money to deal with that situation. My mother worked at the bar, and I got the job of taking care of my father and the new baby plus the three other siblings. I can see the Lord's hand in all of this as I look back because my father proved them wrong and did start walking again.

My uncle put a pulley on the ceiling over his bed, and he exercised all day long with a rope around his legs and arms. I got the privilege of feeding him the food I cooked, and it was a bad scene. He thought that I was trying to poison him. After several months of this routine, my uncle would carry him out and set him on a chair under a tree, and he kept exercising his arms and legs. Then my uncle brought a horse and tied my father into the saddle, and he rode the horse eight hours a day. This gave me more freedom.

Another terrorizing time of my life was the 1959 earthquake that happened that summer after Kitty was born and before my father's accident. I was home with the kids and trying to be the tough one for them, but I almost lost it.

The next day, I went to my private place, which was a huge tree in the brewery park. I climbed to the branch that was so large a kid could lie on its branch and watch the sky. At that moment, there was an aftershock that was strong enough to almost throw me out of the tree. That was the last time I spent time in that tree. I felt so alone that I began calling out to a god that somehow I knew existed.

In Hebrews chapter 8 to 10 and 11, it says, "I the Lord will put My laws into their minds and I will write them upon their hearts and I will be their God and they shall be My people." The Lord puts it into all persons' hearts to hunger for him. Many people try to fill that need with everything but the Lord. It took years for me to overcome the damage that that terrorizing time did to me. Soon after the earthquake happened, a group of people came to the school and gave me a little new testament, which I kept under my pillow, and felt much comfort from it. I did try to read it.

Of course, the school now was in partitions in the gym as our school was damaged so badly by the earthquake. I attended the seventh grade in the gym. There were partitions that separated the first four grades from the fifth through eighth grade, and the upper half of the gym was used as the high school. The school was repaired in time for my last year in grade school. There were, at the most, five students in my grade all the years of my schooling.

My father was well enough from his accident that he was given the job of janitor at the school when I was in the eighth grade. We kids went with him to help do the cleaning. That was the first time I'd ever seen a boys' bathroom and remember being shocked at the difference between the girls' and the guys' rooms. I learned how to do a good job of cleaning that year. My father wasn't a marine for nothing. And he did make a good sergeant. I have to say that the girls' bathroom lost the competition over who was the cleanest.

I remember eighth-grade graduation. I received some gifts, and one of the gifts was a purse. My sister Sally decided she was going to tease me and take the purse. I took that purse away from her and hit her with it, which split her lip so badly they had to take her to the emergency room in Ennis for stitches. I felt so guilty and ashamed, which just made me act meaner. I had to repent from being so mean to Mickey Brunzelle who was a student one grade ahead of me. He suffered terribly from the 1950s mean girls. My best friend throughout grade school was a girl whose name was Kathy Bowman, who was in my grade. We practiced being mean together. We were the ones who really invented the word *Goth*. We dyed all of our under-wear black, our hair black, and wore only black clothes that year. We started smoking also that year. Kathy wasn't allowed to come to my house, but I sometimes spent time at her house. When her father came home, I hid under her bed until he disappeared. I was terrified of him. He was the undersheriff. He would always say, "Don't you have a home to go to?" I would melt in fear so had to plan when I could go visit Kathy.

The school bus would deliver the Virginia City kids back over the hill from Ennis, and we would spend an hour sitting on the cement ledge in front of the local post office and unwind. I spent time scratching my initials in the cement, which has been a landmark for my kids and grandkids to see in the summers when we did our Virginia City trek on the Fourth of July to see the fireworks.

CHAPTER 16

The boardwalk running through town was our playground. The back doors of all the old buildings where the tourists look in were always opened, and we would go in and clean and play house in the rooms that were decorated like they were a hundred years earlier during off season. We never dreamed that it was called breaking and entering. The place always looked better after we left. We spent much time under that boardwalk collecting the change that people lost that rolled through the cracks. We made big bucks there. It was a good living for a kid. We always had jars of fool's gold to sell to the tourists who were walking on the street, which added to our wage. The generation before called the boardwalk area of town West Virginia, and the kids of that generation weren't allowed to go down there because there were still remnants of a very seedy crowd living down there at that time. I often wonder if those same demonic spirits from that time were never dealt with, which was what caused the perversion of my generation. And maybe after I left they still had free rein, I have walked the perimeter of that town as a Christian and prayed over it the way the Lord directed. And I'm sure that many other believers have done that too.

CHAPTER 17

*L*iving in Virginia City was like living in a large playpen. We were free to run, and we traveled every nook and cranny within a ten-mile radius. The form of discipline we received was a warning to stay out of the mines because they would cave in on us and kill us, which of course we did. Ya right. The sheriff Lloyd Brooks convinced us that there were alligators in the ponds below town and would eat us if we got near them. We knew that there was quicksand because a couple of us and a horse got caught in it. It was interesting to see how my uncle got that horse out of the quicksand. He laid boards on the mud and walked out to the horse and put a rope around his neck, which was the only thing left above the mud and tied that bundle of ropes and chains around the truck bumper and pulled the horse out. The horse lived.

That amazed me. One of the ponds was called the swimming hole, and in the spring, we would skim off the ice in order to go swimming.

Remember those times, Maureen? We lived there in the summer as much as possible also.

Looking to the mountain to the west of Virginia City was a mountain we called Crystal Mountain, which had huge outcroppings of crystal quartz everywhere. We spent much time there finding good samples to sell to the tourists. Looking to the north was Cannonball Hill, which was past the ole dump. The cannonballs were shot from a cannon at the courthouse early in the century, and every yard in town had cannonballs that were found and dragged home for lawnmowers to hit.

The old dump was where we caught baby skunks. I was there but didn't catch any. The older high school boys knew how to deodorize them and made pets out of them. The older boys charged $10 for a deodorized skunk, which amount I never had, which meant I didn't get one. That broke my heart.

Looking to the east was Raspberry Mountain and the granite quarry. We spent much time climbing that hill. Over the top of Raspberry was a flat meadow-like spot, a pond that we thought was a lake and what was left of Jack Slade's cabin. It was all there, just fallen in, and was a great place to play. On the south side of town was Axolotl Lake. I made a trip up to that lake one summer and caught several axolotls and made a place for them to live in a tub at the Pioneer Bar and Bob's Place and at the brewery. I put a cup for tips, and the tourists paid me well for that display. The bartenders took good care of my business.

My uncle rented horses in the summer, and we were the guides. That means most kids who lived in town at different times took their turns guiding. We would round up the horses at seven every morning. I would get up at sunup and go to my uncles' house and lie in the yard until I heard them stir in the house. Then I would go in and be served a wonderful breakfast before we headed to the horse pasture. That was one great thing about my aunt, Dorothy Stephens. She was always willing to feed us if we showed up at mealtime. We would drive the horses through town to the corner where they were tied, saddled, and made ready for the tourists to rent. We learned all the jargon to tell the tourists as we guided them around and showed off on our horses. When it was slow, we would take the horses that we were riding and go to the swimming hole and jump in, horses and all, to cool off. Of course, we all rode bareback, which was a better way to show off. We always fought over who got to wear Uncle Harley's cowboy boots, the old worn-out ones, of course. This couple had two beautiful daughters, Ginger and Janet, who were a great part of our lives also. Working at that horse corral was a highlight of my life, and the tourists loved having kids be their guides. I grew to love the tourists. I was also a born people person and still am. My uncle was a great babysitter of my younger brothers and sisters at that horse corral.

Lester Stiles, who was one of the few true cowboys of his day, had a large stagecoach that was pulled by a team of horses. Tourists loaded into this coach in front of the Bale of Hay Saloon. Anytime there was an extra seat or two after seating twenty tourists, a local kid or two got a free ride. All the local kids fought over who got to ride shotgun, which means in front beside the two drivers. One July afternoon in 1961, the team was frightened by a load of washing that fell out of the back of a panel truck that picked up the sheets and towels that needed washed from the motels and cabins that were rented in town to the tourists. The horses ran away and pulled the stagecoach over the side of the hill off the main road over huge boulders, down onto the back road, throwing all the tourists out and killing one lady. The horses finally dumped the stagecoach on the back street after taking out the picket fence in front of my grandfather's house. The horses didn't survive that wreck, and the stagecoach was destroyed.

Chapter 18

$\mathcal{S}$ally, my sister two years younger than I, was my closest friend when we were kids. Of course, she had that white blond hair and beautiful blue eyes. I had ratty-looking light brown hair and yellow brown eyes. She was a natural people magnet. She went through worse things than I did growing up but always had and has to this day a smile from ear to ear and such a positive outlook on life.

Jon, my younger brother, was our doll. Sally and I dressed him like our baby and put him in a buggy and pushed him all over town. We even pushed him off the library/museum lawn in the wintertime, and Jon and the buggy landed in a snowbank down on the highway. He survived us. Karla was the most beautiful sensitive little blonde girl of us all, whom we all convinced was adopted. She lived and grew up without too many hang-ups to our amazement. And she is still that beautiful little blonde girl.

Kitty was the town's little girl. Someone always salted the pay phones with change in the bars for Kitty to find. When she laughs to this day, her eyes sparkle, and she makes a person just feel like they have been touched by an angel. It was always said that she looks the most like me, the lucky girl.

My aunt Dorothy Stephens owned one of the two grocery stores, and we could always depend on her to fix soup for us in her makeshift kitchen at the back of the store when we got hungry. We had a running charge account at the grocery. When my parents got behind in keeping it paid up, we got cut off from charging groceries. At those times, it was fine with us. We just showed up hungry at the store usually at noon and had what she fixed for lunch so it worked. She also hired us to act like tourists and watch for thieves who came into the store to steal her knickknacks that she had for sale. What a life. We thought we were so important. When the grocery business slowed down in order to make a living, the mercantile also became a feather flower shop. Anyone who was willing to spend an hour or two in that store got a job of wrapping and making flowers to be put into bouquets, and these flowers were shipped all over the country.

CHAPTER 19

*O*ne summer, we found a nest of baby magpies, and I personally owned two of these birds who lived in my bedroom. We heard that if a person slit these birds' tongues they could be taught to talk. I didn't slit their tongues, but I did try teaching them to talk. That was an ongoing project. They only lasted for that summer and then disappeared. I also had a pet owl named Henry. We found him as a baby, took him home, and he also lived in my bedroom. Several people in town thought that he was their bird, but he lived with me so he was mine. My window was always opened; in fact, it was broken out, and these birds could fly in and out as they wanted.

I also had two pigeons that also lived in my bedroom. I wonder if I had fleas. My mother talked my brother into taking the pigeons to Sheridan and dumping them out, but when he did, they made their way back to my bedroom, which made me think that they were homing pigeons. They only lasted one summer too and then disappeared. When I went downtown, my owl Henry would fly out of my window and land on my shoulder until he got so big that he had to walk beside me. We would walk around town, go into the bars, and the owl thought he owned the place. When he got tired, he disappeared; and when I got home, he was always there in my bedroom waiting for me.

One summer, my older brother Pete came with two of his brothers to spend a few months. I was on the street and saw a fifteen-year-old boy across the street and knew who it was. I ran across the street and yelled, "Are you Pete's brother?" He said, "Yes, are you Pete's sister?"

Someone commented to me who heard that and said it just made them laugh. I have thought about that so much as Matt and I became dear friends, and he has always been a dear brother. Matt, I will never forget you. Pete's brother Fred was also a fantastic addition to our house, which was always trashed. I think Matt and Fred didn't care. They loved it. I was always looking for the perfect mother, and the many young mothers who moved into town had the gift of me on their doorsteps anytime I could get away. If I needed a special dress for a school function, I could always depend on a lady whose name was Faye. I once borrowed a beautiful blue dress from her, and I wore it to shreds. Another lady whose name is Iris was always there for me, and in her wreck of a life, there was always time for me. She prayed for me and actually led me in the sinner's prayer, which I'm sure was the start of my hungering for a relationship with Jesus.

Someone built a little shop that sat by the post office that became what they called the Horn House. They used deer horns to make puzzles, lamps, and trinkets and displayed them on little shelves for the tourists to buy. I was one of the kids who got the job of tending shop and selling the merchandise. The owner taught us how to do the puzzles of rings tacked onto a deer horn with a metal part that was weaved through the rings. That was a great tourist attraction. We sold these puzzles like candy. Of course, we also sold candy cigarettes and other weird kinds of sweets.

I went to work in the local cafés and as a host for the Virginia City players in my early teens and just let the younger kids start fending for themselves.

During the centennial in 1963, I finally got an identity. I was voted to be the Virginia City Centennial queen. I still have that beautiful red gown that my aunt had made for me.

I loved this freedom of being a teenager and decided it was time to be on my own at age fifteen. I was sure that I was grown up, could take care of myself, and needed a change for my life.

CHAPTER 20

I moved to Sheridan and found a place to live and worked for my board and room and attended school there. I can honestly say that I was a true homeless person leaching off anyone who would let me. I stayed with three different families that year. Faye my earlier wannabe mother, had just gotten married and let me live with them for a short time. Then I moved on to Barb and Gary's house and learned much about what a normal family looked like. She was a tiny little lady who looked like a million dollars. The worse thing there that I did was steal a girdle from her, which caused me to have guilt for years before I told her what I had done and asked for forgiveness.

I had a dear friend whose name was Marie Brunzelle and a cousin whose name was Skippy McClurg who had twenty-inch waists, and these two girls wore waist cinchers to give them fifteen-inch waists. I was sure that that girdle would make me look skinny and beautiful like those two. What a farce that was. I threw that girdle out soon after. I didn't know how anyone could ever wear something like that. I couldn't take all the pain that it took to look beautiful.

Now back to the story of my move to Sheridan. Another lady whose name was Geraldine had five sons and a husband who was never around. Geraldine asked me to stay and help her. I stayed at her house for the rest of the school year.

I met my husband John in Sheridan, and we eloped March 6, 1964. We drove to Idaho Falls, Idaho, because there wasn't a waiting period there. I was seventeen for five days, and John was nineteen. Of course, he had to make false IDs for ourselves because we were too young to be legal. John doctored up two driver's licenses that he found that said I was twenty-one and he was twenty. When we got to Idaho Falls, we found the courthouse but found out that we had to get blood tests. That scared the holy you-know-what out of me. I asked John to drive around the block so many times that we almost ran out of day to get the job done. I finally got the guts to go into that hospital and get a blood test then to the courthouse for the license. By that time, it was 5:00 p.m., and we didn't know where to go to get married. We decided to go to a movie called *The Ugly American* instead. What a boring movie. I still can't tell you anything about it. We were driving down a one-way street the wrong way, and a man in a car yelled at us to warn us of the dilemma. We ended up knowing him as he was from Twin Bridges. We went roller-skating with him and his wife. They lived in a train car; that was all I remember about them. We ended up back at that courthouse the next morning, and the judge and his secretary stood up for us and married us.

John worked for the Union Pacific Railroad, and we lived for the first few months in a section house at Red Rock. After a few weeks of marriage, John ended up in the hospital with pneumonia, and I was so young that I didn't know that I had a right to be in his room. I thought that I had to sneak in to see him, and I lived in the car that I didn't know how to drive and wandered the streets for four days waiting for him to get well enough to get released from the hospital. Oh, how naïve a young girl can be.

When we were married, I had a new issue to deal with. I was addicted to Virginia City and the freedom of running and doing whatever I wanted, and now I walked into a new life of staying home and submitting to a husband. I really meant those words that I had to repeat when we got married, but it was a hard one. For better, for worse in sickness and in health, for rich or poor till death do us part.

And after almost fifty-four years of marriage, they can't say that our marriage is illegal I hope.

We had our first of three wonderful sons when I was still seventeen and John was barely twenty.

Harold Jon "Jay" was born on October 15, 1964. If you count back, you will find that we did what the generational curse always causes. Premarital sex is a sin against yourself and is a high price to pay. But babies are always a blessing, and Jay was the light of our life and both families' lives because he was the first grandson in both families. His name was Harold because both grandfathers' names were Harold.

Of course, I remembered the responsibility that I was rebelling from when I abandoned my brothers and sisters, and they all became part of the package when John married me. The youngest sister Kitty was barely four years old, and she felt abandoned when I moved to Sheridan. They all spent much time at our house. John also was a young kid whose father had been killed in a car accident the year before, and he had a younger brother whose name was Mike and sister Diana who needed caring for. His mother was a lost case, or so I thought at the time. We later became close friends. She also came to know Jesus as well as the brothers and sisters.

After I married John, we went to visit his uncle who was a dentist. I was horrified when he wanted to check my teeth. Then he was horrified and begged me to let him pull the rotten ones. When he was done with me, I had twelve teeth left, and they have stayed in great shape ever since; the day of aching teeth and swollen-up cheeks from infection were over. Praise God. There really is a God, and dentists aren't from the devil. I forgot to tell you that when I was a homeless person, I had such a terrible toothache and swollen-up face that I walked into the local dentist in Sheridan and he told me that he had to pull the rotten culprit. He acted very disgusted, which made me feel so low that a person would have had to dig me up to bury me. But I was so sick that I had to let him do this to me. I saw that dentist go into the other room and take a big swig of what I thought was whisky because that was how it was done where I lived, but now I'm sure that it was just breath freshener. He gave me a shot that was supposed to numb my face, but evidently, he didn't wait long enough for it to take effect. When he started pulling, I thought he was trying to tear my head off so I grabbed his hands and tried to get him to stop. I was screaming. He put his knee on my lap and was stronger than me and kept pulling and yelling at me to get my hands off him. The tooth finally popped out, and he yelled at me to "GET THE HECK OUT OF HERE!" I ran out of there and vowed to never go back to a dentist. He was so mad that I never got a bill.

Hmmmmmm. Maybe he didn't know where to send the bill, as I was a homeless person living under a bridge. So now you know why I didn't trust John's uncle. He promised me that he wouldn't hurt me. He didn't. But I got four dry sockets and almost died of pain a week later. When that dentist found out that I was pregnant, he was horrified and drove to Sheridan from Dillon to check on me and give me antibiotics. The only reason that I lived through this was because God had other plans for me and Jay. The day of infected teeth was over. That infection that I had all my life didn't kill me because of God's plans for the next generations.

We moved to the ranch into a small trailer house soon after we got married to begin our new life. John's older brother, whose name was Jim, owned that trailer and owned a 1959 Buick car, which John and I took over the payments for. I don't have to even tell you the stress of living next to a mother-in-law who was as crazy as a loon, and I'm not kidding. And having a husband who had to work a full-time job elsewhere before coming home to do the ranch work was pretty scary. I spent much time visiting anyone who would allow me to. I spent time at Larry and Wanda Rules when their kids were all preschool kids. She was the best cook and the cleanest house-keeper. I was shocked to see her pull out the stove and fridge to sweep under them when she swept the kitchen. I still don't do that when I clean house. I also spent time at Phyllis Peterson's, learning how to be a good mother. She had a house full of little kids and was in a cast much of the time because of a hip problem. She knew how to fry good round steak for lunch. I visited the Godfreys quite a bit by walking to their house in the late afternoon, and when John dropped Darnell off after work, I would ride home with him. John also dropped Jay and me off at Fay's in the early morning, and we would go to Virginia City for the day, and John would pick us up at Fay's on his way home from work that evening. I did whatever I had to do to not be home when John's mother was around. When I stayed home, I kept the doors locked and didn't answer when she came around as she was always trying to pick a fight, and I didn't know how to handle it. But we managed to get through those years. Barely. When she would get a fight picked and John would come home and find out what she did, I thought World War III had begun. Those two could have screaming fights that would make me shudder. She hated me to the bone. Well, I have to say that I hated her too. Thank God we all grew up and forgave each other for the pain we all caused.

John's mother moved away when she got married. John went to college and then began teaching school. I became the rancher who got to stay home and take care of the sheep and the cows. I learned very quickly how to do the lambing and the calving. I had some neighbors whom I could call on when I was having trouble with a cow who was having trouble calving. We learned many tricks on how to make the job easier. When spring arrived, my kids rode a million miles with me brushing the fields. If the weather got too cold, sometimes the tractor wouldn't start, and we would have to load a wagon by hand to feed the cows.

One day, I accidentally put a pitch fork tine through the hand of John's brother Mike. It went into the palm and stuck out through the back of his hand. I don't think that he even went to the doctor, but it healed okay. My kids tell stories of the wagon tire running over their foot and incidents that I shake my head at. One day, Kip was riding on the seeder as John was planting the field, and his legs were flopping around until he got his leg caught in the steel wheel. He screamed loud enough then John heard him and got stopped before tearing off his leg.

CHAPTER 21

*W*hen Jay was a few months old my grandmother Hazel Barber was moved to the Sheridan Hospital from California because she was dying of uterine cancer. Jay and I rode the school bus to town and spent the days with her as she was dying. She loved that little boy who crawled around her bed most of the day before we left to catch that bus for home. I inherited her Bible after she died and I always love the scriptures that she underlined. I couldn't understand the rest but reading what she underlined made me feel close to her.

My grandmother came to visit the summer before she got sick. She loved John. I remember John and me driving her to Butte to take the plane back to California. We were going over Harding Way, which is the mountainous highway that goes over the continental divide. It has many steep sharp turns going down the side of the mountain. My grandmother was sitting in the front with John, and I being many months pregnant was sitting in the backseat. I got carsick and nervous, but my grandmother thought it was a great ride. She enjoyed every minute she had with us. It was amazing that she died in the same room at the hospital in Sheridan as my mother and then John.

CHAPTER 22

*W*hen our oldest son Jay started first grade, John decided to quit his job on the railroad and began attending college in Dillon. I went back to high school by attending night classes in Twin Bridges. Of course, we had $350 in the bank, so I had to find odd jobs fast. We milked a cow and sold the milk. I babysat kids and wrote the weekly gossip for the three newspapers. We also ran the local theater in Sheridan, which was in the large building between the gas station and the Doug Smith Office. What a hoot that was.

I loved the teenage kids. They all hung out at the theater. If they didn't have any money to get in, they would work in the front until the movie was half over and then go in to watch the rest of the movie. The kids would chew tobacco and spit it on the floor or in cups that would spill over when we swept the place after the movie. There was always a pile of kids who stayed and helped me clean, which was their ticket to get in free. I warned them about chewing and spitting. One seventh grader I will never forget told me that he chewed but never spit. He swallowed it. I couldn't believe it, but he proved it to me. He always was there to help sweep up. Charley Rossiter was one of my favorite little kids. He could sweep that place faster than any kid I knew when the movie was over. There were many times we took kids home all the way to Alder because it was twenty below zero, and they hitchhiked to get around.

CHAPTER 23

*T*he first year of John's college was also when I got the flu, or so I thought, for three months. Our second son, Thomas Joseph, was born on Friday, June 13, 1969. You would think that I must be pretty dumb to not know what was happening, but I didn't because of health issues.

A year later, another baby was on the way. When I was almost six months pregnant with this baby, the doctor informed me that there was not a heartbeat and I would have to pack a dead baby until my body naturally went into labor. I carried him for a month, and finally the day arrived, which was June 19, 1970. I almost bled to death. At one point, I could see myself from the upper corner of the room lying on the bed with the doctor and nurse working on my body. I knew that my spirit left my body and I was dying. But something inside me felt a warning that if I died at this time, I would spend eternity in hell. I knew that I would go straight to hell. I began fighting for my life. I will talk about the death of this baby later. From that time on, I had a new calling to find God. I started trying to read the Bible, but couldn't understand it. I did start praying and felt a peace that it was going to be okay.

I also had another problem that was almost too overwhelming to overcome. I was diagnosed with a vicious form of spinal arthritis called ankylosing spondylitis, which was very painful, and the doctor told me that I was headed for a wheelchair at age twenty-three. This genetic disease destroyed my vertebra and fused them together. This infirmity just about devastated me. Another part of this infirmity was ulcerative colitis and a constant inflammation of the eyes called iritis. I refused to succumb to it. But the thought of all the pain I have suffered still makes me cringe.

A year later on July 15, 1971, our third son Kip William was born, and they told us that he had a heart problem. We took him to a heart specialist, and they told us that his aortic valve was deformed and at some time in his life he would have to have it fixed. They told us what symptoms to watch for, and he grew up without a problem. He just wasn't as tough as the other two sons so we spoiled him more to his detriment. We still weren't walking with the Lord at that time and did things like go to the bars to dance.

The night before Kip was born, we were at the club bar dancing. There was an old man whose name was Gus Lueck, who was a great dancer, and I proceeded to dance with him several times. The next day was the day for our son to be born. As I went into the hospital for the nurses to begin the drip, I passed by Gus who was sitting with his wife in the waiting room getting an IV. He asked me what I was doing there, and I told him that I came in to have a baby. He was shocked because of the dancing the night before. It took twenty minutes to have that baby because of my turning up the drip after the nurse left, and when the baby was ready to come, I decided to save the fifty dollars by avoiding the delivery room. I wouldn't let John call the doctor at the time the baby was coming, and Kip was born in the labor room. As soon as they were done taking care of us, I got up, put on my bathrobe, and walked back to the waiting room and told Gus that the baby was here and now I was ready to get dressed and go home. That was the most fun I'd had in a long time. Kip finally did have to have open-heart surgery at age forty. He waited for almost too long and almost ended up on the heart transplant list, but his heart did finally start beating right and he began to mend. Thank God.

Now with three sons and a husband in college, we were still working several jobs to keep food on the table. We would load up kids and head to the theater four evenings a week. John kept the kids up in the projection room as he kept the film going in the camera. I sold the tickets and served the popcorn, pop, and candy down at the front door. I went upstairs one evening to check on the kids and to see how things were going. I found John feeding popcorn to the new baby who was now a few months old to keep him quiet. I tried to stop him from feeding this to the baby, but he said they ate popcorn from the time they were a few months old. Oh well. They lived through it.

One night, when we were playing a movie about Vietnam, Dr. Swager came to take this movie in but had to come out and tell me that my kids were spitting through a peek hole from upstairs and the spit was landing on his head. I thought that served him right for delivering those brats when he did. I had to run upstairs and tell John to control them.

CHAPTER 24

I remember how John would spend his free time in the fall hunting and always had deer and elk hanging ready to be cut up. One morning while cooking breakfast, I heard a loud noise of a gun going off from the bedroom. I ran in to find John in his long underwear with the gun out the bedroom window, and he had shot a six-point buck just below the house. He couldn't be late for school so he told the kids to gut that deer and hang him in the granary and then I would take them to school when they were done. We got that job done in record time.

One year, his brother Mike and Shelley were at the house cutting up elk with us, and we had a fiasco of fiascos. John and Mike were cutting as fast as they could and throwing what meat needed wrapped to Shelley and I to wrap. They got ahead, and we couldn't keep up. Things were getting pretty tense at one point. John came in with a roast to wrap and threw it on the table, so I picked up the roast and threw it out the back door. John went outside and got the huge hunk of meat and brought it back inside and threw it on the table and said, "Wrap it." I pulled out a piece of paper and wrapped that hunk of meat, dirt and all. End of story.

Shelley and I laughed so hard over that situation so many times. She and I became the best of friends. They spent all their holidays here at the ranch with us in that little eight-by-thirty-five trailer. We would have wall-to-wall beds for everyone to sleep, but we had so much fun. We would take day trips over the Gravelly Range or somewhere in the Tobacco Root Mountains or the Ruby Mountains with Shelley and me sitting on the tailgate of the truck while John and Mike would be in the cab taking care of the babies.

I have very wonderful memories of those times of our life, which were good. I was very sorry when Shelley wasn't a member of our family anymore because of a divorce. I cried harder over the loss of her than anything or person I ever lost at that point in my life. Then later as a very young woman, Shelley died of breast cancer. What a terrible loss for her kids and everyone who ever knew her. She had a heart of gold.

When John was going to college and his classes were over for the day, he went to a sawmill that was in business outside of Dillon to work a shift. His pay was enough lumber to build a twelve-by-twenty room onto that eight-by-thirty-five trailer. We got a new living room and bedroom and a huge closet to separate the two rooms. We lived in that trailer for twelve years. Those were good years for us. In the fall, the water would freeze up, which wasn't an issue. We just had to unscrew the hose and bring it in and let it thaw in the bathtub then go hook it back up, and voilà, there was water again. That did get old, and I got pretty sick of winter before it was over. The summer of 1969, Tom was a new baby, and John worked for Babe Lueck hauling gravel to build up the road from the four corners to town. He would haul until about noon and then I would hear him honk from over at the main road, giving me the signal to get lunch on the table. He would drive that dump truck into the ranch and stop to eat then be off again for the afternoon.

As John went to college and then began teaching, I became the one who got the job of lambing and calving. The herd of sheep knew my voice and whistle. They would come running when I went to the corral. There were many cows over the years that needed help with a calf being born, which meant I got the job of figuring out how to get this job accomplished. I shake my head just thinking about the many incidences that happened.

CHAPTER 25

*I*n the early 1970s, Elaine Elser moved to town. Elaine became a very dear friend and mentor, and she knew Jesus Christ. She started a Bible study at her house, and I was invited. We began the first meeting with reading the Gospel of Mark. We held hands and prayed and asked the Holy Spirit to teach us. During that prayer, I felt like I was going to faint from the power of the Spirit of God ministering to me. I knew that I was baptized with the Holy Spirit at that time. I could understand every word we read in the Bible and went home and read constantly. I could finally understand that Bible I had inherited from my grandmother.

No more lying on the couch, smoking cigarettes, and watching soap operas with the kids tearing the house to shreds all day. The Lord totally changed my life. I got John off to school or work, cleaned the house, and read the Bible sometimes eighteen hours a day and prayed and wrote poetry. Jesus is alive and loves me is what I learned. Many of the ladies that came to know the Lord when I came to know him started coming to my house every Tuesday morning and every Thursday morning for Bible study. We each had two or three kids, and there was lots of room for them to run and play. Our kids had built a three-story tree house out in front of our trailer, and the kids spent much time working on that project. Our trailer was so little, and the Bible study got larger and larger to the point of having to stuff ladies wherever they fit. Those days left such good memories for me. Before I came to know the Lord, I had gotten into the habit of treating my kids like I was treated, which was badly, and this came to an end. I learned in the Bible studies that we have value and my values changed.

CHAPTER 26

I also realized that Jesus answers prayers.

I prayed for a house. That was something I thought would be impossible, but we checked out the possibility of getting a loan. Within a month or so, we were building a house.

We had to paint tar on the basement foundation before we could push in the dirt to fill in the hole around the perimeter of the house. I learned a great lesson. (Yes, another tar incident.) I was visiting a neighbor who always had filthy work clothes, and I heard the guy say, "Put my work clothes in the washing machine and add a cup of gas to remove the filth." Aha! There was the answer to my dilemma of the tar on our clothes from painting the foundation. Before I left the trailer for the new house, I loaded the tar-ridden clothes into the washing machine. I added a cup of gas and left. My oldest son came running down to tell us that there was a problem at the trailer. John ran back to the trailer and took care of the problem. He came back and told me I had a mess to clean up at the trailer. I ran up there and walked into a catastrophe. The portable automatic washing machine was sitting there without a lid. It blew off. The clothes in the machine had been on fire as well as the curtains and screens in the window behind the sink. The cupboards almost blew off the wall. They were just hanging loosely, and there was a broken window on the other wall.

Also, we have always had a constant barrage of visitors for coffee, and I had a rack with coffee cups on another wall, which all blew off the wall and every cup broke. I finally had to ask John how in the heck did the clothes fly out of the machine and through the broken window and end up lying in the yard. He said that my son used the sink sprayer to put out the fire on the wall and in the machine, and

69

then John pulled the clothes out and threw them in the yard. The fire on the clothes wouldn't extinguish. I found out that the window just blew out in the explosion. Thank God we didn't have too long left of living in that trailer. The neighbor almost died laughing because he didn't use gas—he used diesel. He said that diesel wouldn't ignite. Twelve years were long enough to live in that trailer anyway. We were almost ready to move into the new house.

But my next dilemma was that John told me that from now on, I could wash the clothes in the bathtub with a scrub board. After a week or two of that, I decided to try something else. I dragged the portable washing machine up to the sink, put the lid back on, and prayed over it and asked Jesus to heal it. He did. The thing worked better than it ever did before. Problem solved.

One day I was sanding the doors to get stained and finished and kept feeling something pulling on my hair. At that time, I had long hair, and what I was feeling was my hair getting caught in the electric sander. At one point, the sander sucked up my hair and it wound up around something inside the case. In a matter of seconds, the sander was held tight against my head and I could do nothing about it. I unplugged it and headed for the hay field where John was mowing down the hay. As I climbed the fence holding the sander against my head, I came upon a yearling calf who got his head stuck in a tree trunk that was split into a V shape. I realized that if this situation didn't happen, that calf would probably have died. I got to the hay field and stopped John as he was going around cutting hay. John had the tools to take that sander apart and unwind my hair out of the inside mechanical parts that caught my hair. Much of my hair was torn out of my head and had to be picked out of the sander. Then John and I went and got the calf freed from the tree trunk. Situations were always happening to us.

We had a milk cow at this time that John milked and I sold by the gallon. One weekend, John went with the Cub Scouts on a camping and fishing trip, and I got the job of milking this cow. I'd never milked a cow in my life. The first day, the job got done, but it took a long time. The second day, I couldn't get the job done and knew if she didn't get milked, it would cause her problems. I called a neighbor who came along with his wife to help me. This neighbor had never milked a day in his life either. We laughed over trying to squeeze those nozzles and get the milk to come out. The cow would swish her tail and hit the person milking across the back of his head, which meant it took a person to hold the tail while a person milked. It took another person to keep the cow from stepping sideways, knocking the person who was milking over and stepping into the bucket. I was ready for John to get home from his camping trip. His excitement was that our son Tom was casting out the fishing line and caught another boy in the ear with the hook. John had just read of a great trick to get a fish hook out without damaging the person. John took the chance of trying to accomplish this trick and it worked. He was famous with the Cub Scouts for what he accomplished.

CHAPTER 27

*T*hings get pretty testy for young couples building houses, and it also did for us. At one point, we got into a terrible fight as we were working on the house, and I had had enough of this strife and contention. I walked back to the trailer that we lived in. I opened the Bible, and the page that my eyes fell on was Haggai chapter 2. I began reading:

> "Who is left among you who saw this house in its former glory? And how do you see it now? Does it not seem to you like nothing in comparison?" (I was feeling so badly that I said, "Yes, Lord, it's not worth it." But I continued reading.)
> "But now take courage," declares the Lord, "and work for I am with you because of the promise I made you, when you came out of Egypt. My Spirit is abiding in your midst. Do not fear," for thus says the Lord. (I did remember the promises he gave me when I came out of my Egypt and how I promised I would allow him to take me through whatever he wanted, if it would help my family and others to come to know him.)
> "Once more in a little while, I am going to shake the heavens and the earth and the sea also and the dry land. I will shake all the nations and the desire for me will come to the people of the nations with this desire the wealth of the nations will come, and I will fill this house with glory. The silver is Mine and the gold is Mine.

"The latter glory of this house will be greater
than the former," says the Lord."
"And in this place I will give peace," declares
the Lord.

I got the message. The Lord wanted this house built, and
through it my husband was going to become a believer.

After reading that scripture, my spirit came alive with hope.
I got back down to the job. I knew after I read that scripture and
allowed the Lord to minister to me it was going to be okay. We got
the house done and moved in, thanks to the help of John Benedict
and his wife Lela who arrived every evening for two months to help
complete the house.

We moved in the week after Easter, and the next six months
were the preparation time that John and I had to get our life back in
order after the two years of the building project, his teaching school,
and us running the ranch. We were exhausted. We lay on the rug and
soaked up the peace and enjoyed having a home large enough to raise
three very active boys.

That first summer was quite an interesting time. We inherited
eight nieces and nephews for the summer and John's mother. There
were kids sleeping everywhere. We bought a trampoline for the kids,
and they all lived on it jumping from morning till evening and then
some insisted on sleeping on it at night. John's brother and family
along with some of their friends came from Indiana in the late summer. John would give the kids rides on the farmhand that we used
to stack loose hay. They loved it. They would get on the teeth, and
John would lift them up as high as the thing would go. The kids all
screamed with delight. We also planted a field of barley and peas that
summer, and the kids spent many hours walking down six-foot-tall
rows eating peas. John would take the canoe up the ditch and let it
off the truck into the water. The kids would spend afternoons riding
that canoe down the ditch, stopping and lifting it over fences, and
riding some more till they got back down to the house.

CHAPTER 28

The following Christmas, our oldest son Jay had an appendix attack and ended up in the hospital. My husband had an encounter with Jesus in the waiting room during the surgery. He had a heart change. The pastor of the church that was birthed out of that Bible study started by the ladies was at the hospital with us. He prayed for John, and John was ready to turn his life over to Jesus. Being strong willed, John slowly changed, but it took handing over issues little by little until we could see the fruit of how Jesus did come in and change him. After twelve years of my husband not talking because he didn't know how to unless it was yelling at the top of his lungs at us, John changed. The Lord did miraculous things for us. Our house became dedicated to the Lord. Our marriage was dedicated to the Lord, and a weekly Wednesday evening Bible study began at our house. Jesus blessed that time of our lives. We had couples come, and they all brought their kids because they could. There were kids everywhere.

The next Christmas, we did the manger scene at our corral with the kids all dressed up. The farm animals were part of the slide show along with kids dressed up as the shepherds, the angels, Joseph, Mary, and the wise men. The horses were even part of the production. One summer, we had a bus filled with kids who were on their way to Mexico from Washington stop and spend a few days. Of course, John spent much of his time doing mechanic work on that bus. The youth group at our house was a blast.

And then the kids all grew up, and we moved on to the next part of our life.

CHAPTER 29

I still had a terrible problem with smoking for the first year of living in our new house. I felt so worthless because I was too weak to be able to quit. Actually, I loved it too much, and it took time to grow to hate it. I love the scripture in the book of Acts chapter 3 about the guy who was lying at the beautiful gate at the temple. He lay there from birth, begging, and Jesus just walked by him when he went to the temple to teach. The meaning of the Beautiful Gate is "in the right time," and the right time for him to get healed was when Peter and John came and said, "Silver and Gold have I none but such as I have, give I thee. In the name of Jesus Christ of Nazareth rise up and walk."

The right time for me to quit smoking was when John began walking with the Lord. The first prayer he prayed was for me to be delivered from smoking. As he was praying, the Lord told him to command a spirit of resentment and a spirit of bitterness out of me. Wow.

I felt that. I had been trying to quit for years so I didn't think that I'd be so lucky as to get free of it now, but to my amazement, I never smoked another cigarette ever again. And I was smoking up to four packs a day. Those two spirits were harassing me for so many years that it felt so wonderful to be free, and they come right out of a spirit of rejection.

Life didn't just turn into an *Alice in Wonderland* story because we had much overcoming to do from our past. I think that it actually took us forty years to overcome the first twenty years of our life from the time we were born.

Chapter 30

*A*fter the Lord delivered me from smoking, I remember driving through Sheridan and smelling a terrible odor coming out from the front door of the Club Bar and Cafe. My smelling senses were so dulled from smoking that I didn't have any idea about how disgusting that odor from smoking and drinking reeked. When I went into that Club Bar/Café that day, the smell in the little foyer leading to two doors, the one on the right to the bar and the one on the left to the restaurant, reeked so badly that I thought a person must have thrown up right there on the floor and I almost did too. This caused me to realize how demonic smoking is because it prepares a person to be opened up to receive an evil entity that comes to entice a person into such bondage. And the drinking I realized was like taking unholy communion. That smell weaving out into the street enticed my parents to not be able to pass a bar when driving through a town. I came to the realization that I almost became the next generation to fall into this trap. I thank the Lord every day for delivering me, and I feel the urge to warn whomever I can to not fall into this trap. It is the destroyer. John and I both came out of homes where alcohol and smoking were a main activity in the family life. We were both born into houses that reeked from secondhand smoke, and our lungs suffered from it. Especially John suffered. He would catch colds that did more and more damage to his lungs. I am sure that we have both had to have sleep apnea masks to be able to sleep through the nights because of the damage to our lungs from our smoking and the secondhand smoke we have inhaled from the day we were born.

Please don't smoke, and if you do, please quit. It will shorten your life, and the golden years aren't very golden if they are spent going to doctors and treating disease caused by smoking. I think back on my young years and cringe as I remember having one of those foul things hanging out of my mouth. I wasn't smoking it. It was smoking me, and the drinking was pickling me. Disgusting, huh? Lord, I repent for damaging my body, which is a temple of the Holy Spirit. Thank you for telling me that what the locust has stolen in my life will be restored and that my life does count for something.

CHAPTER 31

*D*uring those times, our families slowly came to know Jesus one after another. Standing for Jesus at any cost is very important if a person wants to see family come into the kingdom and their lives turn around for the better. We had so many incidences of family trying to get us to do things that Jesus delivered us from. But we didn't get sucked into falling back into our sinful life. We had other issues that we needed to work on, which took a lifetime of work. We finally got it figured out in the last five years.

One fall afternoon, a brother-in-law came to our house for help. My sister left him because of the drinking and the abuse. This brother-in-law tried going to a center that was supposed to help addicts, and it didn't work. I didn't think that it would be that hard to help him. John had to go to bed because he had to go to school in the mornings to teach, but I sat up with this guy all night the first night as he went through the DTs. It was amazing how you could see that demonic spirit of alcohol come out of him. It started from the top of his head, and the nerve endings came to life down his arms and then down his legs and out of his feet. As this was happening, he would start shaking, and I would just put my hand on his shoulder and pray for him. By morning, he had gotten through it and then it was time of being able to instantly jump up in the middle of the night and find him pacing the floor. I slept with my clothes on for a few weeks because of needing to get to the kitchen fast. My brother-in-law and I would sit in front of the fireplace and pray, and he would start talking about the things he had stuffed all his life.

One story he told me was that as a boy, he was babysitting his little sister, and she went to use the outhouse and fell through the hole that adults used down into the refuse and drowned. Jesus did a lot of healing of that man's broken heart from these past memories and delivered him from guilt that he had carried for a long time over what happened with his sister. He spent the winter with us and was restored from what drinking alcohol had done him. In the spring, he moved back to his home and got on with his life, and the Lord restored his marriage. I'm sorry to say that several years later, this man forgot everything the Lord had done for him, and he returned to the old ways of living. In a stupid moment of self-pity, he killed himself, causing his beautiful kids and my sister much grief to overcome. His wife moved on with her life and is now married to a beautiful Christian man. His kids grew up, and are now raising kids of their own but still suffer the loss that happened in their lives.

CHAPTER 32

*M*y father at one point had become such an alcoholic that he was dying. He was blind, couldn't walk, and was sent home from Fort Harrison, the military hospital in Helena, with a destroyed liver and given a death sentence. I began writing daily letters to him, telling him how much I loved him, about Jesus and that he could be healed. I told him if he just died this way he would only leave bad memories for his kids, and if he was willing, Jesus could heal him and get his house in order the right way. He finally made a deal with Jesus, telling Jesus that if he would save and heal him, he would never drink again and he would walk with him the best he could for the rest of his life. My father was healed. My parents divorced after I left home, but my mother called me and told me that my father hadn't had a drink for four days and I'd better get to Virginia City and see him because this God of mine has become part of my father's life and he needed help.

I went to Virginia City and found my father sitting at the kitchen table, very weak but alive. He seemed to have a peace in his heart that I had never seen before. My father didn't even have shoes that fit after what he had been through with swollen feet for so long. Before going to buy him shoes, I had to soak his feet in order to cut his toenails. I thought, My god, no wonder this man couldn't walk. His toenails grew around his toes and were digging into the bottom of his feet. I helped him into the car and took him to the shoe store where we could buy him a pair of moccasins, which were the only kind of shoes sold in Virginia City. Many of my father's friends spent the night partying at the Pioneer Bar a few doors down. We found one of his old friends sitting on the bench suffering from a hangover in front of the shoe store. When this man saw my father, he said that he heard that my father was done drinking and he was going to watch and see if this new way of life would work for my father and, if it did, he was going to try it too. The Lord gave my father five more years before taking him to heaven. He got things right with his kids and with the Lord.

Moving on to the man on the bench is my next story. He did end up dying, but the miracle of his coming to know Jesus was amazing. My oldest son, who finally grew up and moved to Denver, bought us airplane tickets to Alaska. I prayed before we went, asking the Lord to let it be a God trip. We were in Wasilla, Alaska, and I noticed that there was a group that looked like Christians in the city park. We went to see what was happening, and there was a conference going that ministered to a youth group and several hundred people. During an intermission, I went over and began talking to some of the people who were getting ready to serve a lunch. When they heard we were from Montana, they called the youth pastor over. We introduced ourselves and came to find out that he was the son of that man sitting on the bench that my father talked to a few years before in front of the moccasin store. The pastor told us that they were having a session on forgiveness with the kids the night before, and all of a sudden, the pastor began crying to the Lord to show him if his father was in heaven. His parents had divorced when he was a boy. We knew his father, and I told the pastor that I was able to tell his father about Jesus and how Jesus had changed my life and his father had let me pray for him. Then I knew that our trip had eternal value. That encounter gave me a taste for the gifts of the Spirit, which include evangelism, teaching, healing, and so on.

CHAPTER 33

A very dear friend, Cathy Barron, and I started a Bible study for the elderly people in Virginia City who were the group in the bars when I was a child. This Bible study started out with women smoking and drinking beer at the kitchen table while we studied the Bible. They loved all the prayer and love they received, and slowly the drinking stopped and then the smoking stopped. Every old person that I knew of in that town at that time came to know the Lord before they died. I walked those streets and visited every house and prayed for everyone I saw. For me, this prophet was honored in her hometown. Of course, I knew where I would be mocked so I avoided those places. Before driving to Virginia City to do this Bible study, I had chores to do on the ranch. During the spring calving and lambing time, I was amazed how the Lord took care of what was going on at home while I was doing what He wanted me to do in Virginia City. There would be new babies born while I was gone that would be up and eating before I got home. And if any animal needed help, they seemed to wait until I got back. And we never lost any animals during this time. God is good.

CHAPTER 34

*A*fter coming to know the Lord, we attended the Dayspring Mission, and the church was growing with leaps and bounds. Actually, we were some of the first members as the Dayspring was being built. We have many wonderful memories of those first few years attending that church. There were also some terrible times. There was a couple who moved to the area and started attending our beautiful little church fellowship. I loved them so much, and they ministered to me so much. At one point, JoAnne was going to have a baby, which we were all so excited to see born. That baby girl died at birth, and it was devastating to the parents and to us. It totally broke me as past memories came flooding to the surface of the deaths of my brother, sister, and my own baby that died.

I was so broken that I was too helpless to help that couple through their time of grief. In fact, they were the ones who helped me through my time of grief that I had stuffed for years. My brother died of pneumonia because of the propane running out and the house being cold for days. I remember my mother taking him to Butte to the hospital and leaving him there until we got a phone call that he died. As we were driving back to Virginia City from where we were living at the time, I ask my parents what happened, and they just screamed at me to shut up; I and my siblings weren't allowed to discuss the matter ever again. We just pretended that that little boy didn't even exist.

The next winter, another little girl was born. We had moved back to Virginia City, and at the age of eleven, I was in charge of a brand-new baby. One night when my parents came home from the bar, I could hear the baby crying and crying, and I was so angry. Thinking to myself and saying to myself I was off shift. It was my mother's turn to take care of her, and I covered my head and went to sleep.

That is one of the sorriest things that I have ever done because in their drunken state, they put that two-month-old baby in bed with them, and my father lay on her and in the morning my younger sister went into that bedroom and yelled at my parents that they lay on her and killed her. We were told to go to a neighbor's house and a few days later came home to a house without a baby, and we never mentioned her again. We pretended like she never existed. But I didn't get over the guilt and sorrow for all this until the time of the death of the McBlair baby. Then what else came bubbling out of this grief that had been stuffed was my baby who died. When that happened, I came home from the hospital, and we never discussed it again. But in my heart, I thought of him so much. I even named him Ben Andrew. I thought Jay, Tom, Kip and Ben were awesome names. There wasn't the same letter in any of the names.

I didn't have a cent to my name, and the doctor knew that. He asked me if I wanted him to take care of it and avoid a funeral. I at that time thought that his offer was a good idea, and just like an abortion, I constantly worried about what they did with him. I read terrible things later about what they do with babies who died before birth. All of that pain came boiling to a head with the McBlairs' baby girl. I sobbed for a week over that family's loss and the losses that I had suffered. I could finally at least talk about this after that.

I received much healing from these issues at the little church that we attend. I am thankful how the Lord uses others to help us in our need. We only have to ask, and he divinely directs our lives.

CHAPTER 35

I was baptized in the ditch behind the church along with many other members of our little Bible study and the church. Being baptized is a public display of the willingness of a person to change directions and walk how we are designed to walk, coming to know Jesus and becoming the new person and letting the old person that I was fall away. I have always wanted to live for the Lord, which has been a major goal in my life. I learned that giving all and standing the way Jesus would want a person to stand is the way to show unbelievers how to turn their lives over to the Lord also. People watch how we live, which may be the only way the Lord can get their attention. We might be the only Bible that others read. The commandment to honor your parents doesn't mean to lift them up to a place like an idol. The Lord showed me that to honor your parents is to be honorable to the Lord and that honors your parents. That takes away the guilt that I see so many carry. We do measure up to the Lord. We don't have to perform to be good enough. We are His. When we are baptized, that means we leave the old person down in the water and come up a new person. We are part of his body, and he is the one who directs. No more independence. His burden is light.

CHAPTER 36

When a person who knows Jesus Christ as their Lord and Savior prays for their family, the prayers do not go unnoticed by God. There is a releasing of blessing on families.

For some reason, I hungered for the living Savior and called on his name to save me, and He did, releasing me from these generational curses. Of course, I repented for myself and my family line and asked Jesus to heal me and close all doors to all of our past sins.

I pray for protection for my kids and grandkids, my nieces and nephews, from all this past generational garbage. There have been numerous deaths of babies in my family line and untimely deaths that shouldn't have happened. This touched me with the baby I lost. I am so thankful for Jesus Christ coming to deliver me from these things from my family line. I have to be very discerning and watchful that it doesn't creep back in. Prayer and faith releases God's blessing on families. After coming to know Jesus as my Lord and Savior, I was given several opportunities to overcome the issues of abandonment, rejection, and worthlessness that try to hang on.

At one point, Jesus revealed Ezekiel chapter 16 to me, and though it is a scripture pertaining to the Jewish people, it also a Ramah word for me. I read, "The Lord spoke to me and said, You were born in the land of Canaan. Your father was an Amorite and your mother was a Hittite." (When I looked up the words *Amorite*, the meaning is "pride" and *Hittite* means "terror." Those were two demonic forces that I had to deal with in my life.)

> "When you were born no one cut your umbilical cord or washed you or rubbed you with salt or wrapped you in cloths. No one took

enough pity on you to do any of these things for you. When you were born, no one loved you. You were thrown out into an open field. Then I passed by and saw you squirming in your own blood. You were covered with blood, but I wouldn't let you die. I made you grow like a healthy plant. You grew strong and tall and became a young woman. Your breasts were well formed and your hair had grown but you were naked. As I passed by again I saw that the time had come for you to fall in love. I covered your nakedness. Then I made a marriage covenant with you, and you became mine." This is what the sovereign Lord says. "Then I took water and washed the blood off you. I rubbed olive oil on your skin. I dressed you in embroidered gowns and gave you shoes of the best leather, a linen headband and a silk cloak. I put jewels on you, bracelets and necklaces and I gave you a beautiful crown to wear."

What the Lord said to me through this message was all I needed to overcome these issues in my life. I believe the Lord gave me this message, and it would change my life. It was like being kissed by God. Thank you, Jesus.

CHAPTER 37

I 've been thinking about how the Lord deals with us as we live in this fallen world and are constantly being harassed with the enemy of our souls. Concerning health issues, I know that the Lord has used me to pray for different people for healing, and I have seen that happen even with my obvious health issues.

Other times, he protects us as we go through different issues of health problems.

John, my husband, was diagnosed with prostate cancer in the fall of 2010. We spent much time driving to Bozeman for treatments starting in the spring of 2011. This became a ministry in itself. We met many very needy people who were hungry for prayer and the ministry of the Lord. I could go on and on about the miracles that happened. On September 15, John had a doctor's appointment, and they told him that the cancer was in check and he was free for three months. We are praising the Lord for that. During that last year, as John went through the prostate cancer treatment, we have been asked, "Why did God allow that and not instantly heal him?" This is where my thoughts have been today.

I realize that God isn't interested in our having the perfect life where we don't have any problems. I think of the sayings, like "All sunshine and no rain makes the land to become a desert." Our faith and dependence on God has grown so much as we saw how God protected us as we went through that time of John's treatment, and we enjoyed every day of driving two hundred miles per day for nine weeks. We spent quality time with each other. We met wonderful people whom God allowed us to give a hand up to.

We were able to use our gifts of encouragement to others and also gifts of teaching. We went to a naturopath before John's treatment began and learned how to protect his stomach, bowels, and urinary tract from the radiation treatments. We helped several others who were suffering from the debilitating effects that ravaged their bodies from the radiation. John was totally protected from every side effect. We read the Bible and prayed and listened to God's voice as we were on the road. We bought a case of books called *From Prison to Praise*, which we gave out and made available to the others in that cancer waiting room. We left bibles with whoever wanted them and on every table and shelf. We had people just walk up to us and ask us to pray for them, and we told people how to come into a relationship with our loving Savior. It was a blast. This was as close to being the missionary trip that I have always longed to be a part of and was never able to be a part of. The doctors were amazed at how the radiation never touched John, and he was never sick for even a day. It was like the vacation that we never had in forty-eight years of marriage.

I think of Elijah who ran to the Brook Cherith when his situation got too oppressive to rest and God had ravens bring him food. When he was strengthened, he was able to get back into the battle. That is the hand of God protecting. And Noah who was in the middle of a fallen world that had gotten so bad that there was no morality left in the world. People became so wicked that God decided to destroy all living beings. God elected a man named Noah who knew how to hear God's voice because he spent time with God as we all can. God taught Noah how to build an ark large enough to hold all the animals that God would be bringing into that ark to preserve for coming generations of the animals. I have wished many times that Noah would have swatted those two nasty mosquitoes.

Noah called for all people he came into contact with to come in under God's protection, but they just mocked him and went on living like there was no tomorrow. Noah and his family found that there is a place beyond tomorrow where we will be set free from the pain, sickness, sin, and iniquities that people practice. The Lord has made a way to break this curse that goes from generation to generation. Jesus did this for us by being willing to hang on that cross and paying the price for the sins of each and every person ever born. We just have to be willing to hand them over to him. God came through for Noah and his family, and they were safe. He was reaching out for everyone who was there also, but not a person was willing to reach up and take God's hand to get into that ark. He is reaching out his hand right now for all of us. Please reach up and take His hand and get into the ark. There is safety there. Jesus is the ark.

Those people of Noah's day had never seen rain before and didn't believe what Noah was telling them of what was coming. It's the same today. We have to step into the kingdom of God by faith. In Isaiah 5 verse 6, it says God lifts up a banner for us and whistles for those at the ends of the earth. Can you hear his whistle?

Chapter 38

*A*bout five years ago on December 31, John and I were headed home from Butte when our truck was hit head-on by a car that lost control coming down the Butte hill. Someone who was driving too fast through the canyon came down the hill sliding sideways and hit our truck, which was destroyed. But God!

I ended up in an ambulance headed for the hospital because of hurting my neck and shoulder. I received a whiplash and a chest contusion and received a huge black-and-blue arm. This ride in the ambulance was a great time to talk to the person who was taking care of me about Jesus. He realized his need for the Savior, and as we prayed for his salvation, he and I then prayed for the salvation of the others involved in this wreck. It was an amazing time even if I was in such terrible pain. I was released after being checked out and given pain pills and directions on how to take care of myself as I healed. We were able to talk to many people in this world about a god who saves and delivers because of God's divine intervention into our lives. We are here on this earth for such a short time, and then we who are believers will spend eternity doing the things that we love to do without the harassment of the enemy of our souls. Yaaa God.

I asked the Lord why did this happen, and it came to me that if the couple didn't hit us, they would have hit the ditch on our side and there was a chance of them getting killed, which was a good enough answer for me that I am in God's will. I remembered that when I got saved I told the Lord that I would be willing to do whatever he wanted with my life. People have asked me, "How can you believe like you do?" Well, before I asked Jesus to come into my life to save me, my life was such a wreck of constant drama. I was so demonized that I couldn't even stand myself, and Jesus changed my life so much that I would still live like a believer even if it became a proven fact that there was no God because of the change my life took. Just ask Jesus Christ the Son of God, our Savior, to come into your life and save you and change you and make you able to serve him for the rest of your life.

He will do that and it will be good no matter what you go through here on this earth before you get to go to your true home in heaven.

CHAPTER 39

I just read in Genesis 24 about Abraham's servant going back to where Abraham came from to get a wife for Isaac, his son. When the servant got there, he found Rebecca at the well doing the job that she was supposed to be doing, of watering and tending the sheep. She was there at the well at the exact right time to meet the servant of Abraham who prayed for this encounter to happen, for him to know the right girl who was to become Isaac's wife and the one he was supposed to take back to Abraham and Isaac's home.

After spending the night with Rebecca's family and discussing the plan, Rebecca was willing to go with a complete stranger, get on a camel that walks three miles an hour, and go through the desert and the wilderness for five hundred miles to get to where Isaac lived. That had to be a long interesting trip to be riding on a camel at 3 miles per hour. Holy Moly.

The servant must have spent much of that time telling Rebecca all about this new country where he planned to take her and also about this new husband that she was going to be the bride of. When they got there, Rebecca jumped off the camel and ran right to Isaac when she saw him, and they immediately went into the marriage tent and became husband and wife. The servant sounds a lot like the Holy Spirit who is willing to talk to us about who we are and being the bride of Christ and heaven and what things look like there and where we fit in.

The Bible tells us that the Holy Spirit is our Teacher, and we should just spend time in his classroom allowing him to teach us of the Kingdom. This whole story would be a lot to ask of Rebecca. Evidently it was worth it all. I'm sure that you are feeling like your daily experiences are like riding on a camel for five hundred miles through the wilderness, but hang in there because it will be worth it all. Rebecca became famous because of her life of waiting on God. God is using you also and your experiences, so just be patient and enjoy the ride because your experiences together with everyone else's experiences are being weaved together into a beautiful mosaic that will be displayed in the kingdom of God.

CHAPTER 40

Christmas of 2011 was a wild ride.

Well, another year has come and gone and we had a wild ride, but the bronc didn't buck us off. The year started off with John being diagnosed with prostate cancer. Hah! We fooled them. After nine weeks of daily treatments, they couldn't kill him and finally gave up and pronounced him cured. That two-hundred-mile trip per day only gave us another excuse to go shopping at the Home Depot and Lowe's stores. We got so many crazy ideas of how to fix up our thirty-five-year-old house that we had to finally go on a diet. We weren't sure if it was of eating or spending money, but we did it right. John lost twenty pounds, and I gained thirty pounds.

After calving out the cows, feeding the cows, and driving to Bozeman, we ripped out all the rugs in the house and proceeded to put in hardwood floors. And are they ever beautiful. John is a genius. Actually, my brother Jon came down and helped us with those floors, and we could have never gotten them done without him. We appreciate him so much. We then decided to get rid of the 1970s orange counter in the kitchen and put in a lovely gray counter with all the trimmings of travertine on the wall behind and sanded and refinished the cupboards. It invigorated John and exhausted me. Also, a new kitchen window now makes us almost able to watch the cows calve from our stool as we sit daydreaming at the counter we installed.

I love being in my house. John has to bribe me to get me outside. We had a good summer of haying, the best crop we've had in years. And all the cows produced lovely calves that we oohed and awed over until they were put on the truck to go to the sale. John is always brokenhearted to see them go. John loves watching them grow up. This fall, I knew that I had to do something about the extra thirty pounds so was convinced to join the exercise club in town. I have worked out almost daily, and it is paying off. I really think that God plans to see me healed but not the way I had hoped. I am standing up straighter and straighter after being bent over for a quarter of a century. That exercise is the best way I have ever found to deal with pain issues. So I'm feeling over a barrel at times. Sleep in and lie on the couch all day or get on one of those machines and work my you-know-what off. The pain in my neck is a pain in the neck if I don't get out of bed, drive to town, and ride that bronc. He is *not* going to buck me off. I'm going to do this. I'm still trying to convince myself. John goes with me and exercises also. Especially if he thinks I'm starting to get lazy. He really is good company.

We still do play music at church and love every minute of it. I am still the wannabe musician. I have convinced myself to learn the clarinet, the recorder, the cello, and the violin so I do practice them once in a while as John is practicing his guitar. He is also a great singer. I flunked the singing test.

The Lord has been very good to us this year as he always is, so we are happy.

God bless you all and have a wonderful Christmas and a great New Year.

PS: We still have our lovely dog Patches, and he constantly keeps us in stitches. He is the guard dog while we are off doing our thing. He whines at us every time we get home later than he thinks we should. He meets the car, and I swear that he is saying in his whining pitch, "Where have you been?" We feel like teenagers constantly in trouble for not being home on time to pet him and give him treats. Byeee.

CHAPTER 41

Calving Season 2011

$\mathcal{W}$e had three cows left to calve on April 20 and were anxiously awaiting the finish line. One of these cows was a first-year heifer whom we were watching carefully in case we needed to help her out. I went into Sheridan to do a few chores like have a coffee with friends at the coffee shop when my cell phone rang and John was on the other end. He said, "We need to get that heifer in as she is in need of help with calving." So I headed home as fast as I could. We got her into the maternity ward, which consisted of a small pen with an alley for the cow to run down and get caught in a self-catching head catch. As John was working on getting the feet ready to have the chains put on for pulling, I ran and got the piece of equipment that hangs in the shed that hooks onto the chain to assist in the pulling process. (This piece of equipment was the best birthday present I ever got.) It took just a few minutes to have a beautiful baby male calf delivered. He was ready to instantly jump up on his feet, but there was something very interesting going on there with that calf. There was about two feet of small intestine hanging out of the calf's belly button. Yikes! Now what do we do? We called our wonderful vet Doug from the Mountain View vet service, and his wife Ellie was the only vet available at the time so John zipped off his winter coat as it was one of those days that we've had this spring (dang cold).

John laid the coat on the ground, and we put the calf in his coat and zipped it up to protect the intestines. The calf was like trying to hold down like a busy two-year-old. We got the calf into the back of the truck, and John sat with him without a coat as I drove on slick wet roads like a wild man to the clinic about five miles away. When we got there, the calf was taken into the operating room, and we were also allowed to stay and observe the efficiency and amazing wisdom of Ellie the vet at work. She had to clean the spot, shave the spot, keep the guts wet, and start cutting in order to give room to start pushing the guts back in. The guts didn't cooperate like they should so it seemed to be a never-ending battle, but she kept working on them with Dana, Theresa, and the blonde girl all helping and John and I mostly getting in the way—well, actually, I was the one in the way. John was standing back praying for his calf. Pretty soon, Doug got back to the clinic and took over. He inspected the guts to make sure they would work right after they got put back and kept stuffing them in. He had to do some cutting to make room. The calf was on oxygen, or that's what it looked like to me. There were gauges that showed how the calf was doing throughout this time. Doug got the guts in and the calf sewed up and gave him a shot to reverse the medication that put the calf to sleep at the beginning, and all went well.

The next step was me getting into the rider's seat of the truck, and the calf was put on my lap for the ride home to our bathroom, which became the recovery room. We had about one hour before the calf was up, starving and inspecting every area of the bathroom. He guzzled a bottle of first calf milk that has the special immune support that a new calf needs. We realized that if we wanted to get any sleep that night we were going to have to take the calf to the shed. His mother decided that she didn't want to be a mother so the next step of ranching began. For the next two weeks, we had to put the cow in the chute twice a day for the calf to suckle. We also had to take the calf extra bottles of milk a couple of times a day, and he was the hungriest calf I ever saw. He was bonded to John as to his mother. John fell in love with this calf and was sad when he lost his calf to the real mother. It was a great day when the calf started peeing and pooping because we then knew that he was going to be okay. We are so thankful to have such a wonderful veterinary clinic just down the road. We are thinking about adopting Doug and Ellie as our kids since we had to give up the calf to its mother. Isn't God good?

Yes, God is Good.

CHAPTER 42

*I*n the spring of 2014, Johns PSA number started to skyrocket so he was back into the chase of going to doctors. The first doctor was the cancer doctor who sent him to the urologist who discussed tumors in John's good and bad kidney. After a biopsy with no pain med, they sent John to a heart specialist because his heart rate was too low. He wasn't able to have the next step done until he got a pacemaker in. A few months before John had a colonoscopy, the doctor proceeded to send him to Missoula for a breathing mask as he quit breathing while Dr. Shaneyfelt was doing his process in the colon. Now for a pacemaker being put into John's chest right in the middle of below-zero weather in the middle of calving season was an issue. The hospital had to redo the pacemaker because one of the leads came out. John also had to have a stress test at the hospital to make sure his heart was doing okay before doing a cryofreeze surgery of the tumor on the right dead kidney, which was to kill the cancer that was showing up there.

Then after CAT scans, MRIs, blood tests, chest X-rays, we were off to Salt Lake for the removal of the tumor on the right kidney. Then the kidney started to back up so he had to have another surgery to put a stent in the kidney to drain it. Then they had to either replace or remove the stent. John seemed to be just putting in his time to get through all this and back on to living. He had refused to just give up. When they gave him no hope, God told John a different story that he wasn't getting out of this world that easy. They got all the cancer from the kidney, and at that time, the prostate cancer was in check. So we started going into another winter of doing the cow thing again. Calving, feeding cows, and all that comes with that. Another year comes and goes. The next test began the fall of 2016.

CHAPTER 43

*H*ere is my overview of the year in my 2017 Christmas letter.

The Christmas Letter from the Funk Ranch

Well another year is coming to a close and the start of a new life at The Funk Residence. 2017 was our year of spending time at the Cancer center in Butte every three weeks and getting to know and love so many very dear beautiful people. Dr. Marwin and Dr. Eva Curry. The nurses: Melissa, Bonnie and Kelli. Marcy was the coordinator.

Last December we made a trip to Seattle to visit the cancer center there and found that the treatment that Butte has was the best. We also spent a few days with my brother Pete and Cathy, enjoying their part of the Washington wonderland. They showed us the area and took us to delicious eating places, and their beautiful daughter Jamie who is married to their son John gave us the tour to downtown Seattle by driving from Shelton over every road that is imaginable from back alleys to little side streets which brought us to the Seattle cancer center.

They took us to our Dr. Appointment and left us to spend the night at the cancer centers house. We then we went to the airport the next morning for our trek back to Montana via Salt Lake City. Now this was the vacation of a lifetime. We had an unforgettable trip. Our truck was sitting in 2 feet of snow at the Butte airport waiting for us to come and rescue it. After sitting for most of the day in Salt Lake because of the weather there finally was an opening over Missoula for the plane to be able to land because of the terrible weather so the plane made a quick run from the Salt Lake Airport for the airport in Missoula on the other side of Butte. There were 2 tracks for the plane to land and also 2 feet of snow there. We were shuffled by a 28 seat bus from Missoula back to Butte on the worse roads I have ever seen. There were 61 people on the plane and I don't know how many people were stuffed into that bus but we got to sit in the very back practically on the luggage. We just turned it all into a great adventure. Singing and laughing and getting to know each other were what were on the agenda. Getting to Butte was a miracle. And getting home on those roads was a greater miracle. Now for a year of driving on those roads back and forth to the Butte Cancer center was the next step through the middle of calving season and feeding cows again. John's chemo started after the first of the year.

Calving season began in the middle of it all. John bought a calf catcher that hooked alongside the 4 wheeler. That thing was amazing. He got all the calves caught and tagged with-out getting killed. We both got the flu in the middle of Calving season so the cows were pretty much on their own. We survived that. Then we had the field to get ready to plant so I was amazed to see the plowing, disking and planting get done. We poured five cement culverts to put into the ditches to help with the irrigating which helped tremendously. By the 4th of July weekend John was feeling pretty puny. Many of our family members and some that we didn't know we had come to visit that week and spent the time with us. It was sweet.

The kids jumped right in and helped with the first cutting of hay. John kind of revived for the second cutting and we got it done. He slowly went downhill with each chemo in the fall. I was amazed how he got into the tractor and got the ditches closed up for the winter. Then the kids took turns being here and getting the rest of the fall work done. We got the calves sold the first part of November and John started making arrangements for getting the cows sold. He knew that he wouldn't be able to keep on with the work that the cows required. On the day after thanksgiving I had to call the ambulance to come get John. That night he graduated and went to heaven. I am so thankful that he didn't have to linger on and on. He was ready to go to heaven.

Jay and Barb and the kids were with us when this all happened and it was a time of great sorrow but so happy that Johns time of pain was over. John trusted the Lord in every situation. He was the easiest most thankful patient I have ever seen. I had to help him with everything that needed done for him the last month. I learned so much.

I've never been very touchy feely in my life but helping him get into bed at night, tucking him in and kissing him and telling him I loved him was good for both of us.

As the time got closer for him to go to the Lord I got the privilege of tucking him back in and repeating the whole process every hour or two all night as he needed to sit up or turn or whatever. He never complained about anything. Every morning I would read him the daily Bible reading in the one year Bible. He loved to hear me read to him. I always had a book going that I would read to him. He always prayed over every meal and never missed praying for his kids, Grandkids and great grand-

daughter and for the friends from church and for whoever was in a difficult situation. Also we always had someone who came to visit and would end up eating with us. John would pray for them too.

I heard one of the nieces say that when Uncle John prayed for the food if it was too hot it was just right by the time he got done. He was a prayer who received wisdom from God.

Those were sweet times. Now the cows are gone and I am resting up from my year of driving and caregiving.

I have no idea what God plans for me but I know that it is going to be good. Next week is Christmas and the reason for the season is that Jesus was born in a stable and raised up to be the salvation of all of us.

Which reminds me of a song that speaks to me. It goes like this.

"And if I be lifted up He said will draw all men to me.

I raised my eyes to the skys ahead and His love lifted me.

Reach up to Him. He is reaching down to you.

You could never sink so low don't you think God knows what you're going through.

The miles of space His amazing Grace will span.

Reach up to Him. Reach up and take Gods Hand.

That is what I have done and it's all good. Thank You Jesus.

Chapter 42 is a good one to end this story on. Psalms 42:8 says, "Every day the Lord pours His unfailing love upon me, and through each night I sing His songs, praying to God who gives me life."

Isiah 40: 31 says,

They that wait upon the Lord shall renew their strength.
They shall mount up with wings as eagles.
They shall run and not be weary. They shall walk and not faint.

Teach me, Lord. Teach me, Lord, to wait. You are coming soon.
Tell everyone to look up and to God's hand.

About the Author

Sue Funk was born and raised in Southwestern Montana by alcoholic parents who opened the door to a world of dysfunctional neglect and abuse. She suffered great loss as a child along with her siblings, but her story celebrates the change of six generations of family because of being willing to call on a god of hope and restoration. She allowed Psalms 68:6 to become a reality in her life. In her neediness, she chose to allow God to position her into the family as the solitary who leads in bringing others out of bondage. She stood as a doorkeeper for the house of the Lord and refused to dwell in the tents of the wicked. She came to believe that the Lord her God would be her shield and would give her grace and glory.